AIR FRYER COOKBOOK

"The Italian Way".
120 Effortless Italian Recipes with Color Pictures for Beginners and Advanced Users.
Instructions, Tips and tricks.

COPYRIGHT 2022
ALL RIGHTS RESERVED. NO PART OF THIS PUBLICATION (*WITH THE EXCEPTION OF PHOTOGRAPHS*)
MAY BE REPRODUCED, DISTRIBUTED OR TRANSMITTED IN ANY FORM OR BY ANY MEANS, INCLUDING
PHOTOCOPYING, RECORDING OR OTHERWISE.
IN ANY FORM OR BY ANY MEANS, INCLUDING PHOTOCOPYING, RECORDING OR OTHER ELECTRONIC OR
MECHANICAL MEANS. WITHOUT THE PRIOR WRITTEN PERMISSION OF THE PUBLISHER
EXCEPT IN THE CASE OF SHORT QUOTATIONS INCORPORATED IN CRITICAL REVIEWS
AND CERTAIN OTHER NON-COMMERCIAL USES PERMITTED
BY COPYRIGHT LAW.

TABLE OF CONTENTS:

1 Aperitif Snacks and delicacies

Alpino cheese with red fruits 11
Avocado and egg tartlets 13
Bites of bacon and prunes 7
Bread and cheese omelette 22
Crispy feta cheese with soft heart 24
Delicious croissants "Cornetti" 10
Fried potato gnocchi 14
Fried ravioli with sausage and peppers 6
Fried shrimp triangles 19
Garlic mushrooms 8
Mini sausages in puff pastry 15
Mouthwatering ham rolls 25
Panissa genovese "Fried chickpea bites" 20
Potato croquettes "Crocchette" 12
Ricotta and basil balls 9
Ricotta and zucchini "Crocchette" 16
Salty muffins with zucchini and ham 23
Savory pumpkin and walnut cupcakes 17
Stuffed Ascoli Olives 21
Yogurth flatbreads "Piadine" 18

-

2 Vegetables and side dishes

Accordion Potatoes 29
Baked puree puffs 30
Breaded artichokes 41
Brussels sprouts with shallots 34
Cauliflower gratinated 42
Chips with yogurt sauce 28
Courgettes scapece with mint 39
Patatine" with garlic 27
Potato Millefeuille 37

Quick stuffed peppers 35
Rainbow Veggies 33
Ratatouille 32
Roasted asparagus 31
Roasted corncobs 38
Stuffed Courgettes 36
Stuffed mashed potatoes "Surprise" 26
Stuffed pumpkin flowers 40

-

3 Meat specialities

Beef Bites with Red Martini 86
Beef tenderloin with prairie mushrooms 80
Bites of chicken breast 44
Cashew nut and ginger chicken 55
Chicken (or turkey) steaks with Marsala wine 54
Chicken "Saltimbocca" 53
Chicken burgers "Panino al pollo" 45
Chicken cubes with herbs "Aromi" 51
Classic lamb chops 72
Crispy green curry chicken wings 48
Crispy sesame chicken 56
"Diavola" chicken wings 43
Duck Breast in Balsamic Sauce 49
Duck with berries 50
Exotic pork 60
Farmer's Chops 76
Fiorentina steak 87
Glazed chicken 47
Green pepper fillet 79
Lamb meatballs with Parma Ham 71
Lamb tenderloin in puff pastry 74
Lamb with potatoes and peppers 75
Leg of lamb with white wine 73
Liver Venetian style 77

Milk turkey 52
Mouthwatering meatballs 85
Pork cordon bleu 64
Pork meatloaf 65
Pork mushrooms and cream 67
Pork tornadoes 61
Red Martini Beef 84
Red wine sausages "Salamelle" 62
Roast beef in pink dot 83
Roast Pork 63
Roast pork skewers 66
Roasted pork neck 58
Roasted pork ribs 57
Rosemary-flavored chops 68
Sausage rolls with garlic and rosemary 59
Spiced chicken thighs with marinade 46
Stewed leg of lamb 70
Strawberry lamb 69
Stuffed pockets 81
Veal escalopes with prosecco wine 78
Vitello Tonnato 82

-

4 Fish and Seafood

Calamari with stuffed heart 103
Crispy calamari 99
Crispy salmon fingers 98
Inked cuttlefish 91
Mussels au gratin with pecorino cheese 93
Prawn quick skewers 101
Roasted Sea Bass 100
Salmon with dill 94
Scallops gratin 102
Sea bass baked in foil 97
Sicilian Fried Stuffed Sardines 90

Simple codfish "Baccalà" 88
Tuna Ligurian style 92
Walnut-crusted salmon 89
Warm shrimp and prawn salad 95
Whole-grain salmon gratin 96

-

5 Sweet Cakes and Biscuits

Big milk donut "Ciambella" 110
Blueberry muffins "Tortini" 105
Burnt Coffee Cream 111
Caprese Cake 113
Carnival fritters "Frittelle" 115
Cocoa and Chocolate Drop Cake 108
Cocoa and hazelnut cookies 119
Coffee italian cheesecake 114
Cream burned 109
Crunchy hazelnut cookies 124
Dairy biscuits 118
Egg pudding "Budino" 107
Eggless chocolate cookies 116
Italian-style cheesecake 104
Lady's Kisses "Baci di Dama" 122
Peach cupcakes 106
Peanut Cookies 121
Sicilian Almond Pastries 123
Sicilian orange and ricotta cake 112
Spelt and raisin cookies 117
Sweet and savory crumble 120
Walnut cookies 125

-

Nutritional Values, Use of the air fryer, Tips and tricks for cooking 126
Cleaning & Maintenance 128
Standard cooking times 129

I Aperitif Snacks and delicacies

Fried ravioli with sausage and peppers

*Nutritional values:

Total protein 45.9 grams-Total carbohydrates 123.3 grams
Total lipids 44.2 grams-Total calories 1074.5 kilocalories

SERVING 3   PREP. TIME: 15 MIN   COOKING TIME: 10 MIN

INGREDIENTS

4,5 oz/125 g of pork sausage into small pieces
2 tablespoons of parsley
¼ of diced red pepper
1 shallot, finely chopped
7 oz/200 g of pizza dough

INDICATIONS

In a skillet, add the sausage, shallot, and pepper and fry over low heat for 2 to 3 minutes until the pepper is tender. Turn off the heat and add the price. Leave to cool. Preheat the Air Fryer to 200°C/395°F
Using a glass, cut out twenty circles of 5 cm in diameter from the dough. Pour a spoonful of the sausage mixture into each circle. Close the dough with your thumb and forefinger to form a
ravioli. Arrange the ravioli in the basket and insert the basket in the Air Fryer. Set the timer to 10 minutes and cook until golden brown.

I Aperitif Snacks and delicacies

Bites of bacon and prunes

***Nutritional values:**

Total protein 24.0 grams-Total carbohydrates 77.0 grams
Total lipids 28.8 grams-Total calories 663.1 kilocalories

SERVING: 3-4   PREP.TIME: 10 MIN   COOKING TIME : 5-6 MIN

INGREDIENTS

16 pitted dried plums
16 slices of bacon
16 toothpicks

INDICATIONS

On a surface, spread the bacon slices and roll each slice around a plum. Stop with a toothpick.
Preheat the air fryer to 180°C/355°F.
Put the bundles in the basket and cook for 4-5 minutes. Turn and cook for another 3 minutes. Remove from the oven and serve.
Enjoy as an aperitif with a glass of chilled white wine (Prosecco).

I Aperitif Snacks and delicacies

Garlic mushrooms

*Nutritional values:
Total protein 8.1 grams-Total carbohydrates 26.1 grams
Total lipids 3.5 grams-Total calories 168.6 kilocalories

SERVINGS: 2-3   PREP. TIME: 10 MIN   COOKING TIME: 10 MIN

INGREDIENTS

1 slice of white bread
Freshly ground black pepper
1 clove of crushed garlic
12 mushrooms (champignon type)
1 tablespoon of finely chopped parsley
Salt
Olive oil

INDICATIONS

Preheat the Air Fryer to 200°C/395°F. Grate the bread into very fine crumbs using the food processor. Mix the breadcrumbs with garlic, parsley, and herbs and, finally, add the olive oil.
Cut the stem of the mushrooms and fill the cap with the bread mixture.
Place the mushrooms in the basket and insert the basket in the Air Fryer. Set the timer to 10 minutes.
Cook the mushrooms until golden brown. Serve in a serving dish.

I Aperitif Snacks and delicacies

Ricotta and basil balls

Nutritional values:
Total protein 35.4 grams-Total carbohydrates 57.5 grams
Total lipids 35.5 grams-Total calories 690.4 kilocalories

SERVINGS: 4   PREP. TIME: 15 MIN   COOKING TIME: 8 MIN

INGREDIENTS

- 9 oz/250 g of Ricotta cheese
- 0,6 oz/15 g of finely chopped fresh basil
- 2 tablespoons of flour
- 1 tablespoon of finely chopped chives
- 1 egg, separating the yolk and egg white
- 3 slices of stale white bread
- 1 grated orange peel
- Freshly ground pepper

INDICATIONS

In a bowl, mix the ricotta with the flour, egg yolk, 1 teaspoon of salt and pepper. Then add the basil, chives, and orange peel. Divide the mixture into 20 equal parts and, with moistened hands, create balls. Leave to rest for a while. Using the food processor, reduce the slices of bread into very fine crumbs and add the olive oil. Pour the mixture into a deep dish. Lightly beat the egg white in another deep dish. Preheat the Air Fryer to 205°C/395°F. Dip the ricotta balls in the egg white and then in the bread. Arrange the balls in the basket, taking care to keep them separate from each other and insert the basket into the Air Fryer. Set the timer to 8 minutes. Cook the balls until they turn golden.

Serve alone or with light orange marmalade.

I Aperitif Snacks and delicacies

Delicious croissants "Cornetti"

Nutritional values:

Total protein 43.5 grams-Total carbohydrates 155.7 grams
Total lipids 107.9 grams-Total calories 1767.3 kilocalories

SERVINGS: 4   PREP. TIME: 15 MIN   COOKING TIME : 25 MIN

INGREDIENTS

14 oz/400 g of ready-made puff pastry
1,4 oz/40 g of cooked ham
1,4 oz/40 g of fontina cheese (or cheddar)
1 egg yolk
Chives to taste.
Salt and Pepper to Taste.

INDICATIONS

Roll out the dough and cut it into 8 equal triangles. Place a square of fontina cheese and a few chopped chives leaves. Put a few cubes of ham and roll up starting from the base to obtain croissants. Slightly bend the tips. Brush the pasta with the egg yolk and cook at 160°C/320°F for approx. 25 minutes. Serve hot.

I Aperitif Snacks and delicacies

"Alpino" cheese with red fruits

*Nutritional values:
Total protein 108.6 grams-Total carbohydrates 40.1 grams
Total lipids 108.9 grams-Total calories 1575.6 kilocalories

SERVINGS: 4   PREP.TIME: 10 MIN   COOKING TIME : 5-6 MIN

INGREDIENTS

14 oz/400 g of "Alpino" cheese, or camembert

3 eggs

Flour to taste

Breadcrumbs to taste

Salt to taste

Compote of red fruit (2,5 oz)

INDICATIONS

Cut the cheese into four wheels. Beat the eggs with salt. Then pass the cheese first in the flour, then in the egg, and finally in the breadcrumbs. Then pass again in the egg and again in the breadcrumbs to obtain a thick covering. Preheat the air fryer at 180°C/355°F for 2-3 minutes. When the air fryer is at temperature, put the cheese in the basket and cook with a splash of oil for 4-5 minutes, then turn and cook 3-4 more minutes to obtain a crisp and golden crust. Serve with a spoonful of jam as a bed. Serve very hot in order to enjoy the creaminess of the melted cheese.

1 Aperitif Snacks and delicacies

Potato croquettes "Crocchette"

***Nutritional values:**
Total protein 35.6 grams - Total carbohydrates 78.8 grams
Total lipids 45.5 grams - Total calories 865.9 kilocalories

SERVINGS: 4　　　PREP.TIME: 20 MIN　　　COOKING TIME : 12 MIN

INGREDIENTS

8,9oz/250 g of potatoes
1,8 oz/50 g of grated parmesan
1,1 oz/30 g of minced ham
0,5 oz/15 g of melted butter
1 egg yolk
Olive oil to taste.
Breadcrumbs to taste
Salt to taste.

INDICATIONS

Boil the potatoes in salted water until cooked. Cool and mash with a fork or potato masher. Add the parmesan, the ham, the butter, and the egg yolk. Make elongated balls, and pass in the breadcrumbs.
Preheat the air fryer to 200°C/390°F.
Place the croquettes on the basket, drizzle with oil and cook for 10 minutes, turning them halfway through cooking.
Make sure you get crunchy breading.
Depending on the size of the croquettes, the cooking time may vary a little.

1 Aperitif Snacks and delicacies

Avocado and egg tartlets

Nutritional values:
Total protein 55.5 grams - Total carbohydrates 42.4 grams
Total lipids 82.3 grams - Total calories 1133.4 kilocalories

SERVINGS: 4   PREP.TIME: 15 MIN   COOKING TIME: 6-8 MIN

INGREDIENTS

- 4 eggs
- 1 avocado
- 4 slices of wholemeal bread
- Grated Parmesan to taste.
- Salt to taste.
- White pepper to taste.
- 4 non-stick greased cups

INDICATIONS

Preheat the air fryer to 160°C/320°F. Toast the bread leaving it for about a minute per side. In the buttered cups, put an open egg seasoned with salt and pepper for each and cook for 4 minutes. In the meantime, with a fork, mash the avocado pulp and season with salt and pepper. Arrange the 4 toasts on a baking sheet and divide the avocado pulp between the slices. Spread with a knife to even out the surface, then place an egg in the middle of each toast. Sprinkle the surface of the toast with plenty of Parmesan cheese and place in the air fryer for approx. 2 minutes at 180°C/355°F. Serve hot.

I Aperitif Snacks and delicacies

Fried potato gnocchi

*Nutritional values:
Total protein 9.5 grams - Total carbohydrates 63.5 grams
Total lipids 5.75 grams - Total calories 327.5 kilocalories

SERVINGS: 3   PREP.TIME: 5 MIN   COOKING TIME : 10 MIN

INGREDIENTS

250 g. small potato dumplings (goodies)
Olive oil qb.
Salt
1 pot with boiling water

INDICATIONS

Preheat the air fryer to 392°F.
Precook gnocchi one minute in boiling salted water, drain.
Place them in a bowl with a tablespoon of oil and mix well. Pour them directly into the fryer basket and cook for 6-7 minutes, halfway through cooking, remove the basket and scout them so they do not stick together. Times may vary from fryer model to model, but will not be more than 10 minutes, in any case taste one from the center to be sure. Remove from the basket and salt, then you can serve.

I Aperitif Snacks and delicacies

Mini sausages in puff pastry

*Nutritional values:
Total protein 41.1 grams-Total carbohydrates 34.1 grams
Total lipids 91.7 grams-Total calories 1125.8 kilocalories

SERVINGS: 3   PREP. TIME: 10 MIN   COOKING TIME : 10 MIN

INGREDIENTS

1 packet of small sausages (about 8 oz/220 g or 20 sausages 1 inch)
1 tablespoon of mustard
3,5 oz/100 g of ready-made puff pastry stored in the fridge or frozen (defrosted)

INDICATIONS

Preheat the Air Fryer to 200°C/395°F. If necessary, drain the frankfurters and dry them with kitchen paper. Cut the puff pastry into 5 strips of 1½ cm each. Cover the strips with a thin layer of mustard. Wrap the sausages in the puff pastry strip. Arrange the sausages wrapped in pasta in the Air Fryer basket. Set the timer to 10 minutes and cook until golden.
Proceed in the same way for the remaining sausages.
Serve them in a serving dish accompanied by a saucer of Italian mustard.

Ricotta and zucchini "Crocchette"

Nutritional values:

Total Protein 34.2 grams Total Carbohydrates 50.3 grams
Total lipids 34.3 grams Total calories 645.1 kilocalories

SERVINGS: 2-3   PREP.TIME: 15 MIN   COOKING TIME : 12 MIN

INGREDIENTS

9 oz/250 g of ricotta

6,5 oz/180 g of courgettes

1,1 oz/30 g of grated parmesan

1,5 oz/40 g of white bread crumbs

Bread crumbs

Salt

Freshly ground black pepper

INDICATIONS

Chop the zucchini in the mixer. Drain excess liquid. In a bowl, combine with the ricotta and crumbled crumbs. Add Parmesan, salt, and pepper; if too wet, adjust with little breadcrumbs. Divide into nine medallions, pass in breadcrumbs. Place on baking paper directly in the basket. Bake at 205°C/395°F for the first 7-8 minutes, then turn and achieve golden brown.

I Aperitif Snacks and delicacies

Savory pumpkin and walnut cupcakes

Nutritional values:

Total protein 48.0 grams-Total carbohydrates 30.1 grams
Total lipids 74.4 grams-Total calories 982.3 kilocalories

SERVINGS: 3-4 PREP.TIME: 15 MIN COOKING TIME : 12 MIN

INGREDIENTS

- 4 eggs
- 10.5 oz grated pumpkin
- 1 oz grated parmesan cheese
- 1 oz of flour
- 3 oz shelled and chopped walnuts
- Salt qb.
- White pepper qb.
- ½ teaspoon sage powder
- 1 tablespoon olive oil
- Muffin molds

INDICATIONS

In a bowl beat the egg vigorously, then add the flour, Parmesan cheese salt and spices, making sure to drain the water well from the grated pumpkin, add it to the mixture, finally put in the oil and walnuts and mix everything well.

Preheat the deep fryer to 395°F. Fill muffin molds about two-thirds full and place directly in the basket. Cook for about 6 minutes, then lower the temperature to 360°F and continue cooking for another 4-5 minutes. Remove from the oven and serve hot. You can serve with a traditional fondue or other sauces to your liking.

1 Aperitif Snacks and delicacies

Yogurth flatbreads "Piadine"

*Nutritional values:

Total Protein 18.4 grams Total Carbohydrates 96.6 grams
Total lipids 5.9 grams Total calories 512.8 kilocalories

SERVINGS: 4   PREP.TIME: 10 MIN   COOKING TIME : 3-4 MIN

INGREDIENTS

4.2 fl oz of yogurth

3.8 oz of flour

1 pinch of salt

1/2 teaspoon baking soda or non-vanilla baking powder

INDICATIONS

In a bowl mix the ingredients, then finish kneading on a floured surface. It will turn out soft and slightly sticky. Cut the mass into 4 equal balls, flattened with plenty of flour to a thickness of 2-3 mm. In the deep fryer at 395°F cook one at a time or all at once if you have a large model. Cook 1-2 minutes per side. Let cool and stuff to taste. You can open them like a kebab bread and stuff them or fold them over the filling. Once stuffed you can eat them or reheat them to melt any cheese or chocolate etc.

Great for an endless variety of snacks. They can be prepared in minutes.

I Aperitif Snacks and delicacies

Fried shrimp triangles

Nutritional values:
Total protein 34.8 grams-Total carbohydrates 129.7 grams
Total lipids 16.9 grams-Total calories 809.4 kilocalories

SERVINGS: 3-4   PREP.TIME: 15 MIN   COOKING TIME : 10 MIN

INGREDIENTS

4.5 oz of shelled and shredded shrimps
2 tablespoons of parsley
2 tablespoons of tomato sauce
A splash of chili pepper
1 shallot, finely chopped
7 oz of pizza dough
Salt qb.
Olive oil to taste.

INDICATIONS

In a skillet, put the shrimp the sauce and shallots and sauté over low heat for 2 to 3 minutes with a little oil. Turn off the heat and add the parsley and chili, season with salt, and then let cool. Preheat the air fryer to 395°F. Cut twenty 2-inch squares out of the pizza dough. Pour a tablespoon of the shrimp mixture into each one. Close the dough with thumb and forefinger, forming triangles. Arrange the bundles in the basket and place the basket in the air fryer. Set the timer to 10 minutes and cook until golden brown with a splash of olive oil.

I Aperitif Snacks and delicacies

Panissa genovese "Fried chickpea bites"

Nutritional values:

Total protein 16.7 grams - Total carbohydrates 43.36 grams
Total lipids 10.01 grams - Total calories 335.25 kilocalories

SERVINGS: 4   PREP. TIME: 15 MIN   COOKING TIME: 12 MIN

INGREDIENTS

2.6 oz of chickpea flour
7.6 fl oz of water
1 pinch of salt
Olive oil to taste

INDICATIONS

Steep the chickpea flour in the water with a whisk, stir well to remove all lumps. Pour the mixture into a small saucepan over low heat and stir while cooking so it does not stick to the bottom, at boiling it will begin to harden, when it has consistency (10-12 minutes approx.) pour it into a baking dish so that it is approx. 1 inch thick. Let it cool well, then unmold it from the baking sheet and cut into sticks or 1 inch squares. At this point preheat the fryer to 375.F and arrange the squares spaced apart, drizzle a little oil and start cooking, cook for 4 minutes then gently turn them upside down and drizzle with oil, cook for another 4-5 minutes until crispy golden brown.

I Aperitif Snacks and delicacies

Stuffed Ascoli Olives

*Nutritional values:

Total protein 48.1 grams-Total carbohydrates 56.6 grams
Total lipids 54.4 grams-Total calories 907.6 kilocalories

SERVINGS: 4   PREP.TIME: 15 MIN   COOKING TIME : 8 MIN

INGREDIENTS

3.5 oz of chopped cooked ham
2 eggs
1 oz of breadcrumbs+ as much as is required for breadcrumbs
20 pitted giant green olives
1 oz of Grated Grana cheese
Salt and pepper to taste.

INDICATIONS

In a bowl mix the prosciutto with one egg the grana cheese and 1 oz of breadcrumbs, a pinch of pepper and create a smooth soft but malleable mixture. Carve the olives on one side and fill the pit hole by filling to slightly widening the olives and reforming the roundness with an excess of filling. Beat the remaining egg with a little salt and pepper, dip the olives and then coat them in breadcrumbs. Preheat the fryer to 355°F. Place the olives directly in the basket and spray with a little oil . Cook for 6 to 8 minutes, taking care to shake the basket once or twice. during cooking to even out the browning. Serve hot.

I Aperitif Snacks and delicacies

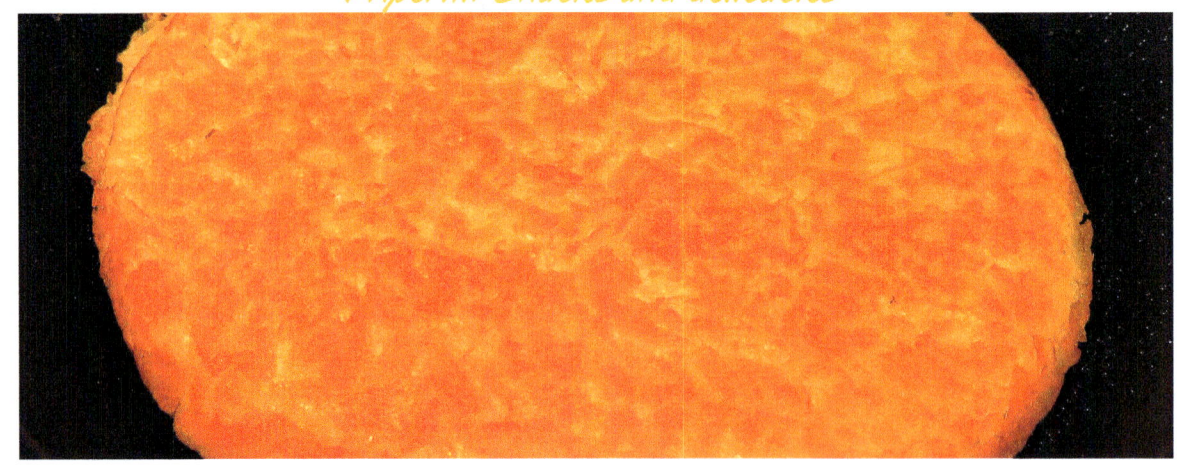

Bread and cheese omelette

Nutritional values:
Total protein 82.9 grams-Total carbohydrates 81.7 grams
Total lipids 67.0 grams-Total calories 1261.1 kilocalories

SERVINGS: 4 PREP.TIME: 10 MIN COOKING : 20 MIN

INGREDIENTS

- 8 eggs
- 3.3 fl oz of milk
- 4.3 oz of cubed stale bread
- 2,5 oz grated pecorino romano cheese
- 1/2 teaspoon garlic powder
- Salt to taste
- Olive oil to taste.
- 1 baking pan

INDICATIONS

In a bowl, beat eggs with salt pecorino cheese and garlic. Cut the bread into small cubes (removing the crust) and soak in the milk, let soften. Preheat the air fryer to 350°F. In the bowl of eggs, add the softened, hand-cracked bread, squeezing it slightly before incorporating. With a whisk, mix well, taking care not to leave large pieces of bread in the mix. Pour the egg mixture into the pan and cook for approx. 20 minutes. Serve cut into wedges or squares with a tease in each piece as an appetizer.

1 Aperitif Snacks and delicacies

Salty muffins with zucchini and ham

Nutritional Values:

Total protein 58.5 grams-Total carbohydrates 22.7 grams
Total lipids 42.1 grams-Total calories 704.3 kilocalories

SERVINGS: 4   PREP.TIME: 15 MIN   COOKING TIME : 12 MIN

INGREDIENTS

4 eggs
2 small courgettes, grated and drained
1 oz of grated parmesan cheese
0,7 oz of flour
3 oz of cooked ham in strips
Salt qb.
Sweet paprika qb.
1 teaspoon chopped chives
1 tablespoon olive oil
Muffin molds

INDICATIONS

In a bowl beat the egg vigorously, then add the flour, parmesan cheese salt and spices, making sure to drain the water well from the grated zucchini add them to the mixture, finally put the oil and ham cut into small strips and mix everything well. Preheat the fryer to 395°F. Fill muffin molds about two-thirds full and place directly in the basket. Cook for about 6 minutes, then lower the temperature to 355°F and continue cooking for another 4-5 minutes. Remove from the oven and serve warm.

I Aperitif Snacks and delicacies

Crispy feta cheese with soft heart

Nutritional values:

Total protein 47.8 grams-Total carbohydrates 19.7 grams
Total lipids 60.7 grams-Total calories 816.6 kilocalories

SERVINGS: 4   PREP.TIME: 10 MIN   COOKING TIME : 10 MIN

INGREDIENTS

One 9 oz slice of feta cut it in 4 pieces
1 teaspoon dried oregano
1 teaspoon dried thyme
1/2 teaspoon garlic powder
2 eggs
Breadcrumbs to taste
1 nonstick baking pan

INDICATIONS

First you will need to soak the cheese in fresh water and leave it for 15-20 minutes. This will allow the feta to release some of the salt, as it is already very salty. In a deep dish, beat the egg. Mix the spices into the breadcrumbs. Preheat the fryer to 350°F. Bread the feta by dipping it in the egg and then in the breadcrumbs; repeat the process to get a thick coating. Arrange the feta in the pan with a splash of oil and place in the basket. Bake for about 10 minutes, be careful: during baking the cheese will acquire a much softer texture, if you should decide to turn it over keep that in mind. You can serve it accompanied by a few canapés of toasted bread and olive pate.

I Aperitif Snacks and delicacies

Mouthwatering ham rolls

*Nutritional values:
Total Protein 54.0 grams Total Carbohydrates 85.0 grams
Total lipids 50.1 grams Total calories 1006.9 kilocalories

SERVINGS: 2-3   PREP.TIME: 10 MIN   COOKING TIME : 7-8 MIN

INGREDIENTS

- 6 slices of cooked ham 3 oz
- 5.3 oz of sheep's milk ricotta cheese
- 2 tablespoons chopped fresh chives
- 1 teaspoon worchestershire sauce
- A few drops of tabasco sauce
- 1 egg
- 2 tablespoons milk
- 1 oz of grated pecorino cheese
- Breadcrumbs to taste
- Salt qb.
- Olive oil to taste.

INDICATIONS

In a bowl mix well the cottage cheese with salt, worchester sauce, tabasco, and chives. Whisk egg with milk and a little salt. Add the pecorino cheese to the breadcrumbs. On a flat surface lay the ham slices, spread an equal amount of ricotta cheese on each slice, leaving 1 inch of ham without filling on the sides. Roll the slices on themselves without pressing too hard. Dip the resulting rolls in egg and then in breadcrumbs. Preheat the fryer to 355°F. When the fryer is hot, place the rolls in the basket and spray a little oil on the surface, cook for 3 minutes then turn them over, spray this side also with olive oil and cook for another 3 minutes.

2 Vegetables and side dishes

Stuffed mashed potatoes "Surprise"

Nutritional values:
Total protein 47.9 grams Total carbohydrates 55.4 grams
Total lipids 51.5 grams Total calories 876.8 kilocalories

SERVINGS: 4　　　PREP.TIME: 25 MIN　　　COOKING TIME : 12 MIN

INGREDIENTS

10,6oz of potatoes

4 slices of cooked ham of thigh

3,5 oz of gorgonzola cheese

2 tablespoons of grated Parmesan cheese

2 tablespoons of olive oil

Salt

8-inches diameter baking sheet

INDICATIONS

Peel the potatoes and boil in water and salt. Mash with a fork to obtain a coarse purée, add the oil and mix well. Line the pan with parchment paper. Spread half of the purée on the bottom of the pan. Stuff with the gorgonzola cheese and the slices of ham. Cover with the remaining mashed potatoes. Sprinkle with grated Parmesan cheese and press lightly to glue it to the surface. Preheat the air fryer to 190°C/375°F. Cook for 10-12 minutes until you get a gratin crust. Delicious as a main dish served with a salad or with good boiled vegetables and sautéed with garlic and oil.

2 Vegetables and side dishes

"Patatine" with garlic

***Nutritional values:**
Total protein 16.0 grams-Total carbohydrates 136.4 grams
Total lipids 19.6 grams-Total calories 786.1 kilocalories

SERVINGS: 4-6   PREP.TIME: 15 MIN   COOKING TIME : 18 MIN

INGREDIENTS

1,6 lb/750 g of yellow-fleshed potatoes
Sea salt
1 tablespoon of olive oil
1 clove of crushed garlic
1 tablespoon of fresh thyme

INDICATIONS

Preheat the air fryer to 180°C/355°F. Wash the potatoes without removing the skin and cut them into thin slices. Dip the potatoes in water for at least 30 minutes. Drain them thoroughly and dry them with kitchen paper.
Mix the garlic, thyme, and olive oil in a bowl and wet the potatoes. Place the potatoes in the fryer basket and insert the basket into the Air Fryer. Set the timer to 20 minutes and fry the potatoes until cooked through and golden brown.
Serve the fries in a warm serving dish and salt them. Delicious as a side dish for tasty meats such as lamb, wild boar, etc.

2 Vegetables and side dishes

Chips with yogurt sauce

*Nutritional values:
Total protein 26.5 grams - Total carbohydrates 146.4 grams
Total lipids 31.7 grams - Total calories 976.5 kilocalories

SERVINGS: 4-6   PREP.TIME: 15 MIN   COOKING TIME : 20 MIN

INGREDIENTS

- 1,1 lb/500 g of large yellow-fleshed potatoes
- 2 tablespoons of finely chopped parsley
- 2 julienned onions
- ½ tablespoon of olive oil
- Freshly ground black pepper
- 0,3 pt/150 ml of Greek yogurt

INDICATIONS

Wash the potatoes without removing the skin and cut them into strips with a thickness of 8 mm. Soak the potatoes in water for 30 minutes. Drain them thoroughly and dry them with some kitchen paper. Preheat the Air Fryer to 150°C/300°F. Dip the potatoes and the onions in the oil before transferring them to the basket Fryer. Insert the basket in the Air Fryer and set the timer to 5 minutes. Pre-fry the fries until tender and crunchy and let them cool. Then bring the Air Fryer temperature to 180°C/355°F. Reinsert the basket with the fries and set the timer to 12-16 minutes. Fry the chips until golden. SAUCE PREPARATION: Mix the yogurt with black pepper salt and olive oil. Serve sprinkled with parsley.

2 Vegetables and side dishes

Accordion Potatoes

*Nutritional values:
Total protein 7.4 grams Total carbohydrates 62.9 grams
Total lipids 8.5 grams Total calories 357.8 kilocalories

SERVINGS: 3   PREP.TIME: 15 MIN   COOKING TIME : 30 MIN

INGREDIENTS

3 medium-sized potatoes 12 oz

Olive oil qb.

Herb salt

1 teaspoon dried thyme

INDICATIONS

Choose three potatoes of the same size so that they are evenly cooked. wash the potatoes well and remove any pods. It will not be necessary to remove the skin. Thread a skewer toothpick through the base of the potatoes so that it is half an inch from the skin; this will help prevent cutting the potatoes cleanly. Now cut the potatoes into thin slices by pushing the knife up to the toothpick, you must create a fan-shaped cut along the length of the tubers. Remove the toothpick and place the potatoes in the basket, drizzle the surface with oil and sprinkle with herb and thyme salt, gently opening the potato slices without breaking them so that the seasoning penetrates between layers. Preheat the fryer to 355°F and cook 30 to 40 minutes depending on the size of the potatoes. Serve hot as a side dish.

2 Vegetables and side dishes

Baked puree puffs

*Nutritional values:
Total protein 35.1 grams - Total carbohydrates 84.7 grams
Total lipids 25.4 grams - Total calories 707.4 kilocalories

SERVINGS: 4   PREP.TIME: 15 MIN   COOKING TIME: 30 MIN

INGREDIENTS

- 0,9 lb boiled potatoes
- 2 oz finely chopped leek
- 1 tablespoon olive oil
- Freshly ground black pepper
- 2 tbsp. Greek yogurt
- 2 eggs
- 1 oz Grated Parmesan cheese
- Salt qb.

INDICATIONS

Boil the potatoes in water and salt and once cooked mashed potato them as for a mashed potato. In a bowl beat the eggs with salt and pepper, add the leek, yogurt, and grana cheese and mix well. At this point incorporate the mashed potatoes in two three times until the mixture is soft but firm. If too liquidy, put in a tablespoon of bread crumbs. Preheat the air fryer to 350°F. In the oiled basket, create balls about the size of half an egg with a spoon or by helping yourself with a pastry bag. Cook for 7 to 8 minutes keeping them an inch apart. When they are ready they will have a crisp, golden crust and it will be easy to lift them out of the basket, while the heart will be soft and creamy

Roasted asparagus

Nutritional values:
Total protein 12.8 grams-Total carbohydrates 11.8 grams
Total lipids 5.8 grams-Total calories 149.8 kilocalories

SERVINGS: 2   PREP.TIME: 10 MIN   COOKING TIME : 12 MIN

INGREDIENTS

0,5 lb medium green asparagus
Olive oil qb.
Salt and pepper to taste.

INDICATIONS

Strip the asparagus of the stem end and peel it from the middle down with a vegetable peeler. Preheat the fryer to 320°F. Arrange the asparagus in the basket steamed with a little oil and with salt and pepper to taste. Cook for 10 to 12 minutes being careful not to burn the tips.
Serve as an appetizer or as a side dish for main dishes, great with two poached eggs.

2 Vegetables and side dishes

Ratatouille

*Nutritional values:
Total Protein 24.6 grams Total Carbohydrates 79.7 grams
Total lipids 10.8 grams Total calories 515.0 kilocalories

SERVINGS: 3-4   PREP.TIME: 15 MIN   COOKING TIME : 15 MIN

INGREDIENTS

- 7 oz of courgettes and/or eggplant
- 2 tomatoes
- 1 yellow pepper
- 2 teaspoons of dried mixed herbs
- 1 clove of crushed garlic
- Salt and freshly ground black pepper
- 1 tablespoon olive oil
- 1 peeled onion
- Baking dish about 6,3 inches in diameter

INDICATIONS

Preheat the air fryer to 390°F. Cut courgettes, eggplant, pepper, tomatoes, and onion into 1 inch cubes. Mix the vegetables in the pan with garlic and herbs, salt and pepper to taste. Add a tablespoon of olive oil. Place the pan in the basket of the air fryer. Set the timer to 15 minutes and cook the ratatouille. Stir the vegetables at least once during cooking. Serve the ratatouille with meats such as an entrecôte or schnitzel.

2 Vegetables and side dishes

Rainbow Veggies

Nutritional values:

Total Protein 25.0 grams Total Carbohydrates 86.4 grams
Total lipids 15.7 grams Total calories 586.6 kilocalories

SERVINGS: 4   PREP.TIME: 10 MIN   COOKING : 12 MIN

INGREDIENTS

1 courgette(large)
1 eggplant(medium)
1 red pepper(small round)
1 yellow pepper(small round)
1 green pepper(small round)
2 white onions(medium)
1 tablespoon olive oil
Salt to taste.
herbs to taste. (basil, mint, oregano)

INDICATIONS

Clean and wash the vegetables. Cut them into medium-sized slices. In a bowl mix all vegetables with oil, salt, herbs. Preheat the air fryer to 395°F. Place alternating sliced vegetables directly into the basket and cook for approx. 12 minutes, stirring two or three times during cooking. Quick and easy, suitable for meat and fish and very colorful. Plate by alternating the different colors.

2 Vegetables and side dishes

Brussels sprouts with shallots

Nutritional values:
Total protein 19.0 grams-Total carbohydrates 22.6 grams
Total lipids 22.9 grams-Total calories 371.5 kilocalories

SERVINGS: 4   PREP.TIME: 10 MIN   COOKING TIME : 15 MIN

INGREDIENTS

1 lb of Brussels sprouts
1 tablespoon olive oil
1/2 teaspoon salt
1 medium shallot, chopped
1 oz of butter
1 teaspoon balsamic vinegar

INDICATIONS

Heat the air fryer to 395°F. Cut the Brussels sprouts in half. Transfer them to a medium bowl, add 1 tablespoon olive oil and 1/2 teaspoon salt, and stir to combine. Place in deep fryer in a single layer. Fry for about 15 minutes, making sure to shake the basket 2 or 3 times while cooking. Meanwhile, prepare shallot butter by finely chopping 1 medium shallot. Place the butter in a medium bowl and melt in the microwave. (Alternatively, melt in a medium saucepan over low heat, then remove from heat.) Add the shallots and 1 teaspoon red wine vinegar and stir to make a smooth emulsion. When the Brussels sprouts are ready, transfer them to the bowl with the shallot butter and stir to combine. Serve hot.

2 Vegetables and side dishes

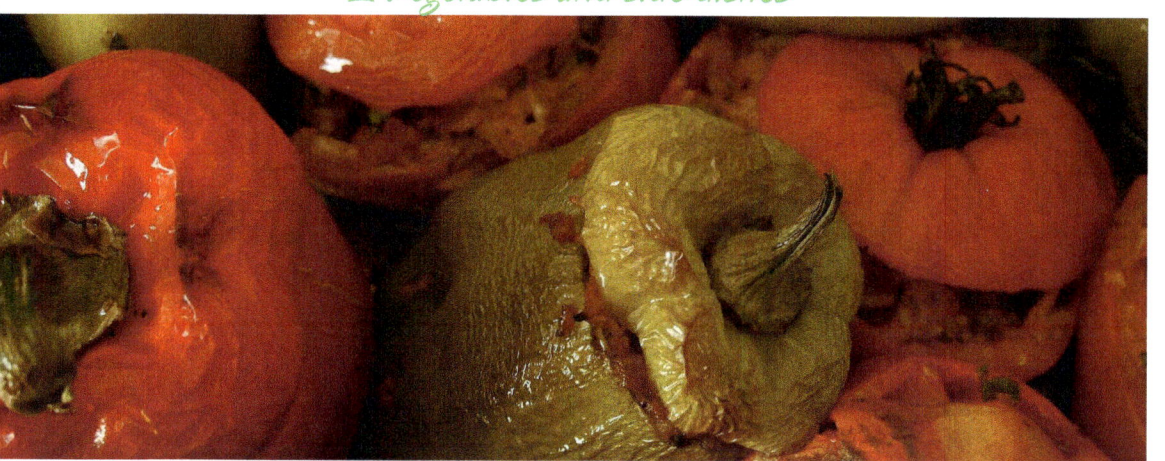

Quick stuffed peppers

*Nutritional values:
Total protein 41.6 grams - Total carbohydrates 101.0 grams
Total lipids 27.0 grams - Total calories 812.7 kilocalories

SERVINGS: 4   PREP.TIME: 10 MIN   COOKING TIME: 15-20 MIN

INGREDIENTS

- 6 peppers (small)
- 4 slices of crustless bread
- 1 egg
- 1,7 fl oz of milk
- 5 desalted anchovy fillets
- 1 oz of Aged pecorino cheese
- 5,5 oz of boiled rice
- 1 clove of garlic
- Salt to taste.

INDICATIONS

Wash the peppers and cut off the cap remove the seeds and filaments from inside. In a blender blend the bacon with the milk, egg the anchovies the pecorino cheese and garlic. Preheat the fryer to 390°F. Meanwhile, combine the rice and spoon fill the peppers, distributing an equal amount of filling in each. Replace the cap by securing it with a couple of toothpicks. If the peppers seem slightly hollow, don't worry a little the filling will swell and a little will flatten the bell pepper, the result will be balanced. Place in the basket with a light drizzle of oil and salt and cook for 13 to 15 minutes, be sure to turn them over a couple of times while cooking.

2 Vegetables and side dishes

Stuffed Courgettes

*Nutritional values:

Total Protein 102.4 grams Total Carbohydrates 14.0 grams
Total lipids 27.5 grams Total calories 712.9 kilocalories

SERVINGS: 2-3   PREP.TIME: 20 MIN   COOKING TIME : 20 MIN

INGREDIENTS

3 zucchini (about 0,9 lbs)
1 whole egg
0,65 lbs of lean minced meat
2 oz of grated parmesan cheese
Freshly ground black pepper
1 clove of crushed garlic
½ teaspoon hot red pepper
Baking sheet or baking paper.

INDICATIONS

Remove the ends of the courgettes and divide them in half lengthwise. Hollow out each half with a teaspoon, forming a small boat about 1/2 cm from the edge and bottom. Season the inside with salt. Recover the flesh from the 'inside by grinding it with a knife and adding it to the filling. Mix the ground meat with Parmesan cheese, garlic, egg, chili powder, pepper and the leftover flesh. Divide the meat into six equal parts. Fill the zucchini slices with the mixture by applying light pressure. Flatten the surface with moistened hands. Preheat the air fryer to 350°F.
Arrange the zucchini in the baking dish and place them in the basket of the air fryer and set the timer to 20 minutes. Cook until the zucchini turn golden brown. Serve on a bed of tomato sauce (photo) or plain.

2 Vegetables and side dishes

Potato Millefeuille

*Nutritional values:
Total protein 62.0 grams-Total carbohydrates 46.6 grams
Total lipids 67.9 grams-Total calories 1044.8 kilocalories

SERVINGS: 2-3   PREP.TIME: 15 MIN   COOKING TIME : 15 MIN

INGREDIENTS

3 medium potatoes (9 oz)
2 oz of Parmesan cheese
5,3 oz of diced asiago cheese
1 oz of chopped walnuts small
salt to taste
pepper to taste
dried rosemary powder qb.
1 baking pan 6 inches in diameter

INDICATIONS

Slice the potatoes very finely with a mandoline and rinse them under plenty of cold water so as to remove excess starch. Line the baking sheet with baking paper and start arranging a first layer of potatoes, sprinkle with salt, rosemary, walnut granules, parmesan cheese and scatter a few cubes of asiago cheese. Continue layering until you finish the ingredients. Spray the surface sprinkled with Parmesan cheese with a little oil. Preheat the fryer to 395°F and bake for 10-12 minutes depending on the number of layers obtained.

2 Vegetables and side dishes

Roasted corncobs

*Nutritional values:
Total protein 27.6 grams-Total carbohydrates 225.3 grams
Total lipids 15.4 grams-Total calories 1150.2 kilocalories

SERVINGS: 2 PREP.TIME: 5 MIN COOKING TIME : 15 MIN

INGREDIENTS

2 cobs
1 tablespoon olive oil
Salt and pepper to taste

INDICATIONS

Clean the cobs and cut them in half lengthwise if necessary. Preheat the fryer to 395°F. Place the cobs directly into the basket sprayed with a little oil and sprinkled with salt and pepper to taste. Cook for about 15 minutes, taking care to turn them over to get the right amount of browning on both sides.

2 Vegetables and side dishes

Courgettes scapece with mint

*Nutritional values:

Total protein 4.6 grams Total carbohydrates 5.8 grams
Total lipids 20.4 grams Total calories 225.2 kilocalories

SERVINGS: 3-4   PREP.TIME: 15 MIN   COOKING TIME: 10 MIN

INGREDIENTS

3 long zucchini (12 oz)
1,7 fl oz of white wine vinegar
2 cloves of garlic
5-6 fresh mint leaves
olive oil qb.
salt to taste.

INDICATIONS

Create an emulsion by mixing 3 tablespoons of olive oil, the vinegar and a pinch of salt. Preheat the fryer to 392°F. Place the thinly sliced courgettes (2-3 mm) directly into the basket, spray with a little oil and a pinch of salt, and cook for 10 minutes, turning a couple of times. Cool a little and then dip the lukewarm courgettes into the marinade, put the mint leaves broken into two or three by hand, mix well and let it season. You can prepare this side dish well in advance; the longer the courgettes stays in the marinade, the more their flavor will be enhanced. If served cold from the refrigerator, they make a good base for mixed appetizers.

2 Vegetables and side dishes

Stuffed pumpkin flowers

*Nutritional values:
Total Protein 80.0 grams Total Carbohydrates 15.1 grams
Total lipids 80.3 grams Total calories 1102.8 kilocalories

SERVINGS: 2-3   PREP.TIME: 15 MIN   COOKING TIME : 8-9 MIN

INGREDIENTS

8 pumpkin flowers
1 egg
9 oz of ricotta cheese
1 oz + 2 oz grated pecorino or parmesan cheese
2 oz of diced cooked ham
2,8 oz of diced fontina cheese
10 chopped mint leaves
Salt and black pepper to taste
Olive oil to taste
1 nonstick baking pan

INDICATIONS

Clean the inside of the flowers and dry them well with baking paper. In a bowl put the ricotta cheese, egg, Parmesan cheese (1 oz), mint, salt and pepper. Mix well. Add the fontina cheese and ham cut into small cubes. Gently with a spoon, fill the flowers with the mixture taking care not to break them. Lay the flowers on the oiled baking sheet and sprinkle with the remaining Parmesan cheese and a few sprinkles of oil. Place the baking sheet in the air fryer at 390°F. and bake for 7 to 8 minutes to obtain a crispy crust.

2 Vegetables and side dishes

Breaded artichokes

*Nutritional values:

Total Protein 57.4 grams Total Carbohydrates 109.4 grams Total lipids 18.6 grams Total calories 835.1 kilocalories

SERVINGS: 2   PREP.TIME: 15 MIN   COOKING TIME : 8 MIN

INGREDIENTS

4 artichokes
Olive oil to taste
breadcrumbs to taste
2 eggs
Salt to taste

INDICATIONS

Clean the artichokes of tough outer leaves and inner beard, cut each artichoke into 8 wedges. Beat the eggs with a little salt and mash the artichokes in them, then coat them in breadcrumbs. Lay them directly on the basket and with a few sprinkles of oil. Bake at 395°F for 8 minutes, turning them once halfway through cooking. They are excellent with a squeeze of lemon juice.

2 Vegetables and side dishes

Cauliflower gratinated

Nutritional values:

Total Protein 26.6 grams Total Carbohydrates 44.7 grams
Total lipids 15.3 grams Total calories 424.1 kilocalories

SERVINGS: 2-3   PREP.TIME: 25 MIN   COOKING TIME: 5-6 MIN

INGREDIENTS

- 10 oz of steamed or boiled cauliflower
- 1 tablespoon of garlic powder
- 2 slices of dry ground bread
- Olive oil to taste.
- 2 tablespoons grated parmesan cheese
- Chili pepper and salt to taste.
- 1 nonstick baking pan

INDICATIONS

Boil cauliflower in salted boiling water and drain while still crispy in a colander. Cool and cut the cauliflower into pieces and season with oil, salt, garlic, chili and bread. Place it on the oiled baking sheet. Sprinkle with Parmesan cheese and brown in air fryer at 395°F for about five minutes. Serve as a side dish.

3 Meat specialities

"Diavola" chicken wings

*Nutritional values:
Total protein 126.8 grams Total carbohydrates 0.3 grams
Total lipids 79.6 grams Total calories 1225.2 kilocalories

SERVINGS: 2-3   PREP.TIME: 5 MIN   COOKING TIME : 12 MIN

INGREDIENTS

1,1 lbs of chicken wings at room temperature
2 tablespoon olive oil
1 level tablespoon of garlic powder
1 level tablespoon of chili pepper
Salt to taste.

INDICATIONS

In a container, pour the olive oil, medium tablespoon of garlic powder the chili powder and salt. Massage the chicken wings with the solution and rest for at least 20 minutes (making sure to wash your hands well so you don't get irritated by the chili). Preheat the deep fryer to 350°F. Place the wings in the fryer basket. Set the timer to 12 minutes and cook, turning occasionally until roasted and crispy. Great with fried potatoes. The spiciness level will be determined by the amount of chili you use; this recipe yields a medium result.

3 Meat specialities

Bites of chicken breast

*Nutritional values:
Total protein 82.6 grams Total carbohydrates 83.7 grams
Total lipids 14.0 grams Total calories 791.1 kilocalories

SERVINGS: 2-3   PREP.TIME: 10 MIN   COOKING TIME: 15 MIN

INGREDIENTS

0,7 lbs of Chicken breast
1 tablespoon olive oil
2 oz of cornstarch
2 oz of breadcrumbs
1 egg
2 tablespoons milk
1/2 tablespoon garlic powder
Salt and pepper to taste.

INDICATIONS

Cut the chicken into cubes; in a bowl beat the egg with 2 tablespoons of milk and dip the chicken breasts in it, let stand for half an hour in the refrigerator.
In a dish mix the cornstarch and breadcrumbs; toss the drained chicken breast bites in the mixture. Preheat the deep fryer to 395°F. Set the timer to 15 minutes and cook the steamed chicken bites with a little oil, turning occasionally until golden brown and crispy.

3 Meat specialities

Chicken burgers "Panino al pollo"

*Nutritional values:
Total Protein 88.4 grams Total Carbohydrates 89.5 grams
Total lipids 21.9 grams Total calories 908.4 kilocalories

SERVINGS: 2   PREP.TIME: 10 MIN   COOKING TIME : 10 MIN

INGREDIENTS

0,6 lbs of ground chicken
1 tablespoon chopped parsley
Salt and pepper to taste
2 lettuce leaves
1 sliced tomato
2 tablespoons mayonnaise
2 hamburger buns
Olive oil to taste.

INDICATIONS

Mix meat with parsley salt and pepper. Preheat the fryer to 300°F and toast the open buns with the center on top for about one minute. Raise the temperature to 360°F. Divide the meat in half and shape into two burgers, which you will cook 3-4 minutes per side with a few splashes of oil. Meanwhile, spread the mayonnaise evenly on the insides of the buns, cover the bottom two halves with the lettuce leaf and tomato slices. Ready the burgers lean on the tomato slices and close with the bun.

Spiced chicken thighs with marinade

*Nutritional values:

Total Protein 149.8 grams Total Carbohydrates 10.8 grams
Total lipids 40.8 grams Total calories 1010.1 kilocalories

SERVINGS: 2   PREP.TIME: 10 MIN   COOKING TIME: 20 MIN

INGREDIENTS

- 4 chicken thighs
- 1 clove of garlic, minced
- 1 teaspoon chili powder
- ½ tablespoon of mustard
- Freshly ground black pepper
- 2 teaspoons brown sugar
- 2 tablespoons olive oil

INDICATIONS

Mix garlic with mustard, sugar and chili powder. Add a pinch of salt and pepper to taste. Mix everything together with the oil. Completely massage the chicken thighs with the marinade and let marinate for 20 to 30 minutes. Arrange the chicken thighs in the basket and place the basket in the air fryer at 395°F.

Set the timer to 10 minutes. Roast until golden brown, then lower the temperature to 300°F and roast the thighs for another 10 minutes until cooked through. Serve the chicken with a corn salad and French bread.

3 Meat specialities

Glazed chicken

*Nutritional values:
Total Protein 173.1 grams Total Carbohydrates 118.3 grams
Total lipids 48.5 grams Total calories 1601.8 kilocalories

SERVINGS: 2-3   PREP.TIME: 10 MIN   COOKING TIME : 15 MIN

INGREDIENTS

6 skinned chicken thighs
5,5 oz of breadcrumbs
1 teaspoon hot paprika
1 teaspoon rosemary powder
1 teaspoon sage powder
1 teaspoon garlic powder
1 teaspoon white pepper powder
2 eggs
3 tablespoons milk
Flour o qb.
Salt qb.

INDICATIONS

In a dish mix all the spices with the breadcrumbs and salt. Separately, beat the egg with the milk. Flour the chicken thighs well, then dip them in the egg and finally bread them with the breadcrumb mix, to get a well-textured breadcrumbs repeat the last two steps. Leave a few minutes to dry, meanwhile preheat the fryer to 320°F.
Place the thighs directly on the basket steaming a little oil and cook for 12-15 minutes depending on the size of the thighs, taking care to turn them in 3-4 minute cycles. Serve with sauce to your liking and potato chips.

3 Meat specialities

Crispy green curry chicken wings

Nutritional values:
Total protein 139.5 grams-Total carbohydrates 0.0 grams
Total lipids 86.6 grams-Total calories 1336.9 kilocalories

SERVINGS: 2-3   PREP.TIME: 5 MIN   COOKING TIME : 12 MIN

INGREDIENTS

- 1,1 lbs of chicken wings at room temperature
- 3 tbsp. olive oil
- 0,4 fl oz of Dry white wine
- ½ tsp. garlic powder
- 2 tbsp. green curry powder
- Salt qb.

INDICATIONS

In a bowl, pour the olive oil, medium spoonful of garlic powder, curry powder and wine. Massage the chicken wings with the solution and rest for at least 20 minutes. Preheat the deep fryer to 355°F. Season with salt and place the wings in the fryer basket. Set the timer to 12 minutes and cook, turning them a couple of times until they are crispy. They can be enjoyed accompanied by crispy chips.

3 Meat specialities

Duck Breast in Balsamic Sauce

*Nutritional values:
Total protein 96.4 grams - Total carbohydrates 8.0 grams
Total lipids 37.9 grams - Total calories 758.7 kilocalories

SERVINGS: 2-3   PREP.TIME: 10 MIN   COOKING TIME: 25 MIN

INGREDIENTS

1 duck breast (about 1 lb)
1/2 glass of balsamic vinegar
2 tablespoons of honey
1 tablespoon juniper berries
Fresh bay leaves
Tarragon leaves
Salt to taste.
Pepper to taste.

INDICATIONS

Using a knife, score the skin of the breast in a checkerboard pattern without cutting through the flesh. Sprinkle the surface with salt and chopped bay leaves, and tarragon. Separately, prepare the cooking sauce, combining honey with balsamic vinegar and a little pepper, and reduce over low heat in a saucepan for a few minutes. Preheat the air fryer to 350°F. Set the timer to 25 minutes. Then place the brisket in the basket after brushing with the sauce, skin side up, and cook for 5 minutes, then turn and brush with the cooking juices (vinegar and honey) and continue cooking, turning and brushing with the cooking juices every 5 minutes. continue the cycle until the skin is golden and crispy. Slice and serve drizzled with the remaining balsamic sauce and decorated with tarragon leaves

3 Meat specialities

Duck with berries

Nutritional values:
Total protein 98.9 grams - Total carbohydrates 27.6 grams
Total lipids 37.4 grams - Total calories 843.0 kilocalories

SEVRINGS: 2-3   PREP.TIME: 20 MIN   COOKING TIME: 25 MIN

INGREDIENTS

1 duck breast (about 1 lbs)
1 orange juice
7 oz of berries (blackberries, raspberries, strawberries, blueberries)
1 tablespoon honey
Fresh rosemary 2 sprigs
Fresh bay leaves 2/3 leaves chopped
Chopped fresh mint leaves (one sprig)
Salt to taste.
Pepper to taste.

INDICATIONS

Using a knife, cut the skin of the breast into checkerboard shapes without cutting through the flesh. Sprinkle the surface with finely chopped salt, rosemary, mint and bay leaves. Separately, prepare the juice for cooking by mixing orange juice, honey and a little pepper. Preheat the air fryer to 356°F and bake the berries with a few mint leaves in a baking dish for a couple of minutes. Turn after a minute and leave for another minute. Remove from the oven and let rest. Then lay the breast in the rack, skin side up, and cook for 5 minutes, then turn and brush with the cooking juices (orange and honey) and cook another 10 minutes, brushing after the first 5 minutes. Turn again with the skin on and brush with juice after 5 minutes and continue for another 5 minutes until the skin is golden brown and crispy. Remove from fryer and rest on a plate, top with berries and leave covered for 5 minutes. Slice and serve with its fruit.

3 Meat specialities

Chicken cubes with herbs "Aromi"

*Nutritional values:
Total Protein 90.6 grams Total Carbohydrates 0.4 grams
Total lipids 7.7 grams Total calories 433.8 kilocalories

SERVINGS: 2-3   PREP.TIME: 10 MIN   COOKING TIME : 10 MIN

INGREDIENTS

0,7 lbs of diced chicken breast
1 teaspoon garlic powder
1 teaspoon thyme powder
1 teaspoon rosemary powder
Olive oil to taste.
Salt and white pepper to taste.

INDICATIONS

Dice the chicken and season with oil spices salt and pepper, leave a few minutes to flavor, meanwhile preheat the fryer to 355°F. Place the chicken directly into the basket and cook, turning every 2 minutes for about 9 to 10 minutes. Having achieved optimal browning and cooking, you can serve on plates with a sprinkle of pepper to enhance the aroma.

3 Meat specialities

Milk turkey

Nutritional values:
Total Protein 86.1 grams Total Carbohydrates 56.1 grams
Total lipids 13.8 grams Total calories 693.0 kilocalories

SERVINGS: 2-3   PREP.TIME: 10 MIN   COOKING TIME: 12 MIN

INGREDIENTS

2 thick slices of turkey breast (9 oz approx.)
Flour qb.
3,5 oz of sliced carrots
1 julienned celery stalk
A few fresh mint leaves
1 bay leaf
1 garlic tooth
1 glass of milk
Salt to taste.
1 baking pan

INDICATIONS

Preheat the fryer to 365°F, flour the turkey and spray with oil, place in the pan with the carrots the celery, garlic and a pinch of salt and cook 2 minutes per side. Lower the temperature to 300°F. Pour the milk the mint and bay leaf into the pan and cook for another 6 to 7 minutes, stirring a couple of times while cooking until you have a creamy sauce. Place on serving plates, on a bed of salad, garnish with the carrots and celery and drizzle with its sauce.

3 Meat specialities

Chicken "Saltimbocca"

Nutritional values:

Total Protein 157.0 grams Total Carbohydrates 117.2 grams
Total lipids 44.0 grams Total calories 1492.6 kilocalories

SERVINGS: 2-3 PREP.TIME: 15 MIN COOKING TIME: 10 MIN

INGREDIENTS

flour to taste
2 tbsp olive oil
3,5 fl oz of white wine
4 thin slices of chicken breast (3,5 oz each approx.)
Fresh sage 8 leaves
1 pinch of salt
4 slices of smoked scamorza cheese
4 slices of prosciutto

INDICATIONS

Preheat the air fryer to 395°F. Lay the chicken on a flat surface, stuff the cutlets in half with ham and scamorza cheese and a sage leaf. Fold them into a pocket to close the filling and fasten with a toothpick. Place the chicken slices in flour and coat well. Spray with a little oil. Place the chicken slices in a baking dish and cook for 3 to 4 minutes. Turn them over and insert the wine. Resume cooking for 5-6 minutes to complete and reduce the wine to make the sauce.

3 Meat specialities

Chicken (or turkey) steaks with Marsala wine

*Nutritional values:
Total protein 163.8 grams Total carbohydrates 59.1 grams
Total lipids 15.4 grams Total calories 1125.0 kilocalories

SERVINGS: 4   PREP.TIME: 5 MIN   COOKING TIME : 10 MIN

INGREDIENTS

4 chicken breast steaks (1,1 lbs)
1 glass of Marsala wine
1 tablespoon of olive oil
Black pepper to taste
2,2 oz of breadcrumbs
1 oz grated parmesan cheese
1 tablespoon dried herbs
Salt qb.
1 nonstick baking pan

INDICATIONS

Place chicken in a container and cover with marsala, let marinate for 30-40 minutes. Mix the breadcrumbs, parmesan and herb mix well.

Preheat the air fryer to 395°F. Drain the chicken and dust well with the breadcrumb mix. Place the chicken in the baking dish directly into the basket of the air fryer, steam with a little oil, bake for 6-7 minutes at 360°F, then bring to 395°F pour the marsala from the marinade into the baking dish and bake for another 2-3 minutes. Serve by drizzling with the cooking juices and sprinkle with pepper.

3 Meat specialities

Cashew nut and ginger chicken

Nutritional values:

Total Protein 112.9 grams Total Carbohydrates 35.1 grams
Total lipids 51.9 grams Total calories 1059.5 kilocalories

SERVINGS: 3   PREP.TIME: 10 MIN   COOKING TIME : 10 MIN

INGREDIENTS

- 0,7 lbs of chicken fillets in strips
- 2,8 oz of cashews
- 1 oz of potato starch
- 1,7 fl oz of soy sauce (less salty version)
- 1 teaspoon of ginger powder
- Olive oil to taste
- 1 baking pan
- 1 carrot
- 1 diced green bell pepper

INDICATIONS

Preheat the fryer to 340°F.
Sprinkle the starch over the chicken strips and mix well along with the ginger as well. Oil the pan with a little olive oil and put in the chicken, cashews and vegetables, start cooking for 4 minutes taking care to turn them a couple of times, at which point add the soy sauce and cook for another 4-5 minutes turning a couple of times. The sauce will have a creamy consistency and all you have to do is serve it.

3 Meat specialities

Crispy sesame chicken

*Nutritional values:
Total protein 90.7 grams-Total carbohydrates 16.1 grams
Total lipids 6.7 grams-Total calories 487.4 kilocalories

SERVINGS: 2-3   PREP.TIME: 10 MIN   COOKING TIME : 10 MIN

INGREDIENTS

1 whole chicken breast (about 10 oz)
1 tablespoon of olive oil
2 oz of sesame seeds
1/2 tablespoon of garlic powder
2 tablespoons of honey
Salt and pepper to taste.

INDICATIONS

Cut chicken into cubes; pour sesame seeds into a bowl, dip the salted and peppered chicken breast into it so that it is lightly coated.

Preheat the deep fryer to 390°F. Arrange the morsels directly in the basket and drizzle with a little oil. Set the timer to 10 minutes and cook the chicken morsels, turning gently a couple of times until golden brown and crispy. Serve drizzled with a few drops of honey.

3 Meat specialities

Roasted pork ribs

*Nutritional values:

Total Protein 238 grams Total Carbohydrates 0.0 grams
Total lipids 762.2 grams Total calories 2270.1 kilocalories

SERVINGS: 4   PREP.TIME: 10 MIN   COOKING TIME : 25 MIN

INGREDIENTS

2,2 lbs of pork ribs
1 sprig of rosemary
2-3 bay leaves
2-3 cloves of garlic
Olive oil
Salt, pepper to taste.

INDICATIONS

Season the meat with oil, salt, pepper, shelled rosemary and chopped garlic and let it season for a few minutes. Place in the basket of an air fryer preheated to 350°F and bake for about 25 minutes. Turn halfway through cooking and check for doneness before baking. There may be variations due to the cut of the meat and the model of the air fryer. Serve with potatoes or tomato salad. Since this is a very fatty meat, you can season it without using oil.

3 Meat specialities

Roasted pork neck

Nutritional values:
Total protein 38.0 grams Total carbohydrates 0.0 grams
Total lipids 20.8 grams Total calories 367.2 kilocalories

SERVINGS: 2   PREP.TIME: 10 MIN   COOKING TIME : 10 MIN

INGREDIENTS

2 medium slices of capocollo
1/2 glass of white wine
2 tablespoons dried oregano
Salt to taste.
Ground black pepper
Olive oil to taste.

INDICATIONS

To avoid smoke, pour some water in the bottom of the air fryer (depending on the model). Soak the meat for 30 minutes with wine and some of the oregano. Drain and massage the meat with oil, salt and pepper. Lay the meat directly on the basket and sprinkle with oregano. Bake at 360°F for approx. 5 minutes. Turn them over and cook at 390°F for another 4-5 minutes depending on the thickness of the meat.
A sprinkling of pepper and oregano powder before serving enhances the flavor.

3 Meat specialities

Sausage rolls with garlic and rosemary

Nutritional values:
Total protein 89.8 grams Total carbohydrates 5.7 grams
Total lipids 108.5 grams Total calories 1358.5 kilocalories

SERVINGS: 2-3   PREP.TIME: 5 MIN   COOKING TIME : 15 MIN

INGREDIENTS

0,9 lbs of Italian sausage
1 teaspoon rosemary powder
1 teaspoon garlic powder
Salt and white pepper to taste.

INDICATIONS

To avoid smoke, pour some water into the bottom of the air fryer (depending on the model). Cut the sausage into two parts, and roll it up forming two wheels stopped with a skewer toothpick. Preheat the air fryer to 350°F. Lay the sausage directly on the basket and steam with half the spices. Cook for 7 to 8 minutes, then flip and sprinkle with remaining spices. Cook another 3 minutes and then raise to 390°F for the last 3 minutes.

3 Meat specialities

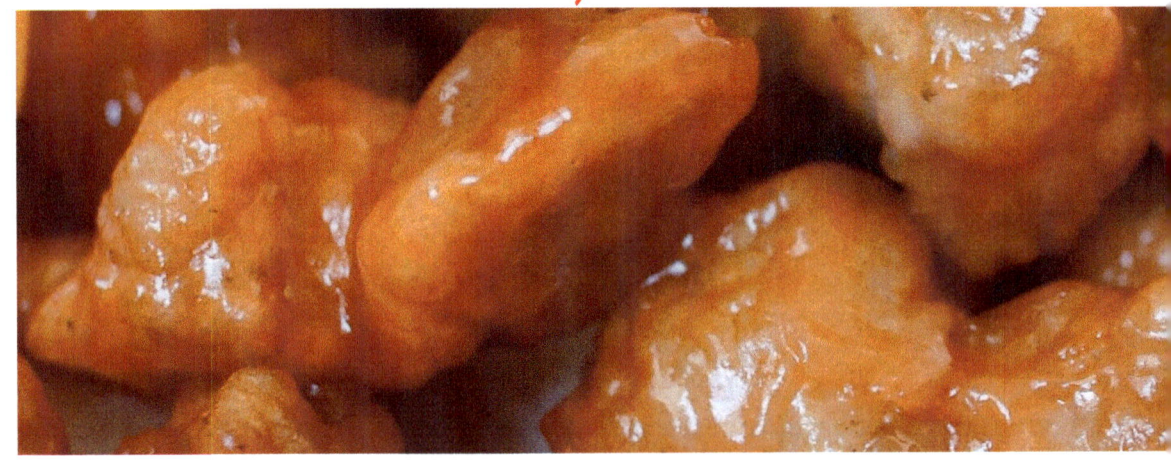

Exotic pork

Nutritional values:

Total Protein 63.4 grams Total Carbohydrates 19.0 grams
Total lipids 26.1 grams Total calories 577.6 kilocalories

SERVINGS: 2-3   PREP.TIME: 10 MIN   COOKING TIME : 10 MIN

INGREDIENTS

10,5 oz of cubed pork loin(1 cm.approx.)
4 tablespoons flour
3 tablespoons tomato sauce
2 tbsp. honey
4 tbsp. apple cider vinegar
4 tbsp. white wine
2 oz of thinly sliced leeks
1 pinch of hot chili powder
Salt qb.
Olive oil to taste.
1 baking dish

INDICATIONS

In a bowl, season the pork with salt, honey, vinegar, chili and a drizzle of olive oil. Preheat the fryer to 340°F. Pass the drained morsels in the flour, sifting well. Pour into the pan spray a little oil and cook for 5 minutes taking care to stir a couple of times, add the white wine the tomato sauce and leek and cook for another 3-4 minutes. Serve hot.

3 Meat specialities

Pork tornadoes

*Nutritional values:
Total Protein 103.5 grams Total Carbohydrates 0.0 grams
Total lipids 50.6 grams Total calories 869.4 kilocalories

SERVINGS: 3   PREP.TIME: 10 MIN   COOKING TIME : 10 MIN

INGREDIENTS

- 6 slices of pork tenderloin (approx. 1 inch thick, 1 lb)
- 6 slices of taut bacon
- ½ teaspoon rosemary powder
- Salt and pepper to taste
- Olive oil to taste.

INDICATIONS

In a bowl, season the tenderloin with a little oil, salt pepper and rosemary. Roll a strip of bacon around each fillet so that it covers the outer edge and secure it with a toothpick. Preheat the fryer to 350°F. Arrange the slices in the basket making sure to leave a space between each one and cook 4 minutes, then turn them upside down and cook for another 3-4 minutes. Serve on serving plates with a sprinkling of pepper.

3 Meat specialities

Red wine sausages "Salamelle"

*Nutritional values:

Total Protein 66.6 grams Total Carbohydrates 0.0 grams
Total lipids 83.3 grams Total calories 1032.9 kilocalories

SERVINGS: 3   PREP.TIME: 5 MIN   COOKING TIME : 12 MIN

INGREDIENTS

0,7 lbs of garlic pork sausages
1 sprig of rosemary
10 juniper berries
1 glass of red wine
Pepper to taste
1 pan

INDICATIONS

Preheat the fryer to 340°F.
In the pan arrange the sausages, on the surface of each piece pierce a few holes with a fork, distribute the juniper berries and flaked rosemary, cover everything with the wine and cook for 10-12 minutes. Serve in small bowls or soup plates sprinkling a little fresh pepper, you can accompany with some croutons or a good mashed potato.

3 Meat specialities

Roast Pork

*Nutritional values:
Total Protein 180.0 grams Total Carbohydrates 23.6 grams
Total lipids 69.9 grams Total calories 1471.6 kilocalories

SERVINGS: 6 PREP.TIME: 10 MIN COOKING TIME : 45 MIN

INGREDIENTS

1 pork hock 1,9 lbs
1 chopped onion
1 sprig of fresh rosemary
½ glass of dry white wine
2 tablespoons olive oil
Salt to taste.
Black pepper to taste.

INDICATIONS

Season the meat by sprinkling it with pepper, rosemary and salt. Place in a roasting pan of a size compatible with the model of the air fryer. Pour in the oil and turn the roast to grease it, then add the onion. Preheat the air fryer to 350°F. Insert the basket with the pan and cook for 45 minutes. Turn the meat halfway through cooking and insert white wine to deglaze . It is excellent served with spicy Italian mustard

3 Meat specialities

Pork cordon bleu

Nutritional values:

Total protein 79.5 grams Total carbohydrates 78.6 grams
Total lipids 46.0 grams Total calories 1045.8 kilocalories

SERVINGS: 2   PREP.TIME: 10 MIN   COOKING TIME : 10 MIN

INGREDIENTS

4 slices of pork loin (7 oz)
4 slices of cooked ham (1,5 oz)
4 thin slices of fontina cheese (2 oz)
1 egg
2 tablespoons milk
3,5 oz of breadcrumbs
Salt and pepper to taste
Olive oil to taste

INDICATIONS

Beat the egg with milk and a little salt in a deep dish. Cut the slices crosswise, opening them like a sandwich, but without separating them completely; leave the last inch of the slice together. Fold the slices open and season with salt and pepper, fill each with one slice of ham and one slice of fontina cheese folded in such a way as to stay inside from the edges of the meat, close the top and press well with the palm of your hand. Preheat the fryer to 350°F. Taking care not to let the filling spill out, coat the cordon bleu first in egg and then in breadcrumbs, sealing the open part well with the breading. Arrange in the basket and steam with a little oil, cook for 4 minutes then turn upside down also steam this side with a little oil and cook another 4-5 minutes.

3 Meat specialities

Pork meatloaf

Nutritional values:

Total Protein 128.0 grams Total Carbohydrates 35.1 grams
Total lipids 40.0 grams Total calories 1013.3 kilocalories

SERVINGS: **4**　　　PREP.TIME: **15** MIN　　　COOKING TIME : **28** MIN

INGREDIENTS

- 1 lb of minced pork leg meat
- 2 oz of ground ham
- 1 tablespoon rosemary powder
- 1 lightly beaten egg
- 1,5 oz of grated parmesan cheese
- Freshly ground pepper
- 3-4 tablespoons breadcrumbs
- 1 small onion, chopped
- 1 baking dish

INDICATIONS

Preheat the air fryer to 390°F. In a bowl, mix the ground meat and ham with the raw egg, bread crumbs, onion, rosemary, 1 teaspoon salt, and a good dose of pepper. Mix everything together firmly. Roll up the meat and form an even roulade. Transfer the meat to a baking dish and drizzle with olive oil. Place it in the basket of the air fryer. Set the timer for 25 to 28 minutes and roast the meat until it is well cooked and golden brown. Let the meat cool for at least 10 minutes before serving. Cut the meat into slices.
Excellent accompanied by a little mustard and served with chips and salad.

3 Meat specialities

Roast pork skewers

*Nutritional values:
Total Protein 181.8 grams Total Carbohydrates 29.5 grams
Total lipids 136.7 grams Total calories 2075.3 kilocalories

SERVINGS: 4   PREP.TIME: 20 MIN   COOKING TIME : 20 MIN

INGREDIENTS

0,9 lbs of Italian pork sausage
0,9 lbs of roast pork
2 courgettes
1 red pepper
1 yellow pepper
1 onion peeled into wedges
1 tablespoon dried mixed spices (garlic, rosemary, pepper)
Olive oil a few sprinkles.
Wooden or metal skewer sticks

INDICATIONS

Cut the meat into squares about 1 inch on a side, the sausage into logs, the peppers into equal-sized squares, and the courgettes into thin slices. In a bowl, mix all the ingredients with the oil and spices. Allow to flavor for a few minutes, then insert alternating sausage, bell bell pepper, meat, zucchini, onion etc. In the air fryer preheated to 360°F, insert skewers and cook for 15 minutes, taking care to turn them occasionally. Bring to 390°F for another 5 to 6 minutes. Serve with a sauce of your choice or with salad or fried potatoes.

3 Meat specialities

Pork mushrooms and cream

Nutritional values:
Total protein 83.5 grams Total carbohydrates 2.8 grams
Total lipids 58.3 grams Total calories 869.8 kilocalories

SERVINGS: 2   PREP.TIME: 10 MIN   COOKING TIME: 10 MIN

INGREDIENTS

- 7 oz of pork tenderloin
- 5 oz of shredded mushrooms
- 1 tooth of minced garlic
- 1 tablespoon chopped parsley
- 1,7 fl oz of Cooking cream
- Salt and pepper to taste
- Olive oil to taste.
- 1 baking dish

INDICATIONS

Preheat the fryer to 350°F.
In the oiled dish put the fillet, the garlic and the mushrooms, salt and spray with a little oil, cook for 3 minutes per side, then add the cream and cook another 3-4 minutes turning the sauce a couple of times. Strain divide in half and plate over the sauce, mushrooms and sprinkle with parsley. This cooking leaves the meat pink, for more intense cooking just increase by a few minutes.

3 Meat specialities

Rosemary-flavored chops

*Nutritional values:
Total Protein 38.0 grams Total Carbohydrates 0.0 grams
Total lipids 20.8 grams Total calories 367.2 kilocalories

SERVINGS: 2   PREP.TIME: 10 MIN   COOKING TIME : 10 MIN

INGREDIENTS

- 2 medium chops
- 1/2 glass of white wine
- 1 sprig of fresh rosemary
- 1 teaspoon rosemary powder
- Salt to taste.
- Ground black pepper
- Olive oil to taste.

INDICATIONS

To avoid smoke, pour some water in the bottom of the air fryer (depending on the model). Soak the meat for 30 minutes with wine and rosemary. Drain and massage the meat with oil, salt and pepper.

Lay the meat directly on the basket and sprinkle with rosemary needles. Bake at 360°F for approx. 5 minutes. Turn them over and cook at 390°F (sprinkle with more rosemary needles), for another 4-5 minutes depending on the thickness of the meat.

A sprinkling of pepper and rosemary powder before serving enhances the flavor.

3 Meat specialities

Strawberry lamb

*Nutritional values:
Total Protein 81.8 grams Total Carbohydrates 10.7 grams
Total lipids 36.0 grams Total calories 694.0 kilocalories

SERVINGS: 2-3   PREP.TIME: 15 MIN   COOKING TIME : 25 MIN

INGREDIENTS

0,8 lbs of lamb fillet
7 oz of diced fresh strawberries
1 tablespoon dried rosemary
1/2 teaspoon ground ginger
Salt and black pepper to taste.
1/2 cup balsamic vinegar of Modena
1 baking dish

INDICATIONS

On the surface sprinkle the fillet with herbs, salt and pepper. In a bowl with a drizzle of oil and salt, season the strawberries. Preheat the air fryer to 360°F. Place the fillet in the pan. Cook by lowering to 340°F for about 10 minutes. Then turn the fillet over and add the strawberries and half the balsamic, then cook for another 8 minutes at 340°F. Bring to 390°F and add the rest of the balsamic. Cook for another 5 minutes. Rest 5 minutes before cutting. This cooking leaves the lamb pinkish. If you prefer it more cooked, simply increase the cooking time by a few minutes. Serve with the strawberries and reduced vinegar base on top.

3 Meat specialities

Stewed leg of lamb

*Nutritional values:
Total protein 373.7 grams-Total carbohydrates 0.2 grams
Total lipids 58.6 grams-Total calories 2022.3 kilocalories

SERVINGS: 6   PREP.TIME: 15 MIN   COOKING TIME : 35 MIN

INGREDIENTS

1 leg of lamb cut into medium pieces (3,3 lbs approx. with bone)
8,5 fl oz of vegetable broth
3 cloves of garlic
1 branch of fresh rosemary
Salt and pepper to taste.
Olive oil to taste.
1 baking dish

INDICATIONS

In a bowl put the meat, broth, a little pepper and a clove of garlic. Let it season for 1/2 hour. Drain the meat and season with salt and pepper, place it in a roasting pan with the chopped rosemary and remaining garlic.

Cook the first 5 minutes at 390°F, then add half the juice from the marinade and cook for 30 minutes at 340°F, taking care to turn the meat every 10 minutes. While cooking, you can add more broth so as not to leave the bottom dry and have a little sauce for garnish. Serve with some of the cooking juices poured over the top.

3 Meat specialities

Lamb meatballs with Parma Ham

*Nutritional values:
Total protein 50.2 grams-Total carbohydrates 31.1 grams
Total lipids 21.6 grams-Total calories 519.5 kilocalories

SERVINGS: 2   PREP.TIME: 15 MIN   COOKING TIME : 8-10 MIN

INGREDIENTS

- 5,5 oz of minced lamb
- One tablespoon of grated parmesan cheese
- 2 oz of ground parma ham
- 1 tablespoon finely chopped fresh oregano
- 1,5 oz of breadcrumbs
- Freshly ground black pepper qb.
- Olive oil qb.
- A baking dish
- Tapas forks

INDICATIONS

Preheat the air fryer to 390°F. In a bowl, mix the ground meat with the breadcrumbs, Parmesan cheese, oregano, parma ham, and black pepper, mixing well. Divide the meat into 10 equal parts and, with moistened hands, form into uniform balls. Place the meatballs in the baking pan and air fryer, drizzle with a little olive oil. Set the timer to 8 minutes and cook the meatballs until golden brown. Serve hot in a serving dish. Also excellent as an appetizer accompanied by slivers of seasoned pecorino cheese.

Classic lamb chops

Nutritional values:

Total Protein 130.1 grams Total Carbohydrates 6.0 grams
Total lipids 22.0 grams Total calories 743.1 kilocalories

SERVINGS: 2-3   PREP.TIME: 10 MIN   COOKING TIME : 12 MIN

INGREDIENTS

8 lamb chops
2 spring onions cut into approximately 0,5 inch slices
1 tablespoon dried rosemary
grated black pepper to taste.
1/2 teaspoon dried garlic
Salt to taste.
Olive oil a few sprinkles.

INDICATIONS

Season the ribs with salt and pepper. Sprinkle with garlic powder and rosemary. Preheat the air fryer to 350°F. Place the chops and onion in the basket. Spray with a little oil and put a little salt on the onions. Cook for 5 minutes, then turn the chops over and stir in the onion. Resume cooking for 5 minutes. Bring to 390°F and cook for another 2-3 minutes, until the surface is golden brown and crispy. Serve with a side salad, great paired with balsamic tomato salad and a few basil leaves.

leg of lamb with white wine

Nutritional values:

Total protein 373.3 grams Total carbohydrates 1.3 grams
Total lipids 58.1 grams Total calories 2054.8 kilocalories

SERVINGS: 6   PREP.TIME: 15 MIN   COOKING TIME : 35 MIN

INGREDIENTS

1 leg of lamb cut into medium pieces (3,3 lbs approx. on the bone)
5 fl oz of white wine
3 cloves of garlic
1 branch of fresh rosemary
Salt and pepper to taste.
Olive oil to taste.
1 baking pan

INDICATIONS

In a bowl put the meat, wine, a little pepper and a clove of garlic. Let it season for 1/2 hour. Drain the meat and season it with salt and pepper, place it in a roasting pan with the chopped rosemary and the remaining garlic. Cook the first 5 minutes at 390°F, then add half the juice from the marinade and cook for 30 minutes at 345°F, taking care to turn the meat every 10 minutes. While cooking you can add more wine so as not to leave the bottom dry and have a little sauce for garnish. Serve with some of the cooking sauce poured over the top. Recommended with a good mashed potato or even polenta.

3 Meat specialities

Lamb tenderloin in puff pastry

*Nutritional values:
Total protein 108.7 grams - Total carbohydrates 63.6 grams
Total lipids 122.7 grams - Total calories 1793.4 kilocalories

SERVINGS: 2-3   PREP.TIME: 20 MIN   COOKING TIME: 25 MIN

INGREDIENTS

0,9 lbs of lamb fillet
1 roll of ready-made puff pastry
1 clove of garlic, minced
3,5 oz of canned liver pate
1 beaten egg
1 tablespoon dried herbs (rosemary, marjoram)
Salt and black pepper to taste.
Baking paper

INDICATIONS

Roll out the puff pastry roll and trim to wrap the fillet without leaving any residue. Spread the liver pate on the puff pastry, sprinkle with minced garlic, then lay the fillet sprinkled with salt and pepper and dried herbs and wrap it with the pastry. Line the basket with baking paper and lay the resulting roll on top. Preheat the air fryer to 360°F. Brush the surface of the puff pastry with egg and start cooking. Cook by lowering to 340°F for about 20 minutes. Then increase to 390°F for another 5 minutes. Rest for 5 minutes before cutting.

3 Meat specialities

Lamb with potatoes and peppers

*Nutritional values:
Total protein 140.5 grams Total carbohydrates 97.7 grams
Total lipids 37.0 grams Total calories 1285.9 kilocalories

SERVINGS: 2-3   PREP.TIME: 10 MIN   COOKING TIME : 12 MIN

INGREDIENTS

8 lamb chops
2 spring onions cut into approx. 0,5 inches slices
1 red pepper
3 medium potatoes diced into small cubes 1cm.approx.
1 tablespoon dried rosemary
Grated black pepper to taste.
1/2 teaspoon dried garlic
Salt to taste.
Olive oil to taste.

INDICATIONS

Season the chops with salt and pepper. Sprinkle with garlic powder and rosemary. Preheat the air fryer to 350°F. Place the chops, onion, potatoes and pepper squares in the basket, spray with oil and put a little salt on the vegetables. Cook for 5 minutes, then turn the meat and vegetables , resume cooking for 5 minutes, then raise to 395°F and cook for another 2-3 minutes, until the surface is golden brown.

3 Meat specialities

Farmer's Chops

*Nutritional values:

Total protein 100.8 grams- Total carbohydrates 80.6 grams
Total lipids 18.7 grams- Total calories 893.7 kilocalories

SERVINGS: 2-3   PREP.TIME: 15 MIN   COOKING TIME: 13 MIN

INGREDIENTS

6 lamb chops (0,7 lbs)
2 red onions sliced about 1 cm thick
½ green celery, (5,3 oz)
6 medium carrots diced small 1cm.approx.
1 tablespoon dry roasting spices
Grated black pepper to taste.
1/2 teaspoon dried garlic
Salt to taste.
Olive oil to taste.
1 baking pan

INDICATIONS

Season the ribs with salt and pepper. Sprinkle with garlic powder and spices. Preheat the air fryer to 350°F. Place the chops, onions, carrots and celery in 2 cm chunks in the pan, spray with oil and put some salt on the vegetables. Cook for 5 minutes, then turn the chops and vegetables, resume cooking for 5 minutes, then raise to 395°F and cook for another 2-3 minutes, until the surface is golden brown. The pan will collect the juices from cooking, use them in the dish.

3 Meat specialities

liver Venetian style

*Nutritional values:
Total protein 64.8 grams Total carbohydrates 28.8 grams
Total lipids 52.8 grams Total calories 890.4 kilocalories

SERVINGS: 2-3   PREP.TIME: 15 MIN   COOKING TIME : 8-9 MIN

INGREDIENTS

0,7 lbs of sliced liver
2 large onions
½ glass of dry white wine
Flour to taste.
Salt pepper to taste.
Olive oil to taste.
1 baking pan

INDICATIONS

Cut the liver into strips about 1 cm wide and coat in flour. Remove the excess with a colander. Cut the onions into thin slices.
Preheat the air fryer to 350°F. Grease the bottom of the pan with oil and place the salted and seasoned onions, then the liver and steam with oil and salt. Cook for 2 minutes and turn. Drizzle more oil over the liver, add the wine, and cook for another 3 minutes. Turn and stir the liver and onions again, return to cook for another 3 minutes. This dish was originally cooked with liver slices, but to adapt the recipe to air cooking it has been modified.

3 Meat specialities

Veal escalopes with prosecco wine

Nutritional values:
Total protein 88.5 grams-Total carbohydrates 23.2 grams
Total lipids 21.4 grams-Total calories 639.4 kilocalories

SERVINGS: 2-3   PREP.TIME: 10 MIN   COOKING TIME : 10 MIN

INGREDIENTS

0,9 lbs of sliced veal
2 tablespoons olive oil
1 clove of garlic, minced
3,4 fl oz white wine (prosecco)
½ tablespoon rosemary powder
Flour qb.
Salt and pepper
1 baking pan

INDICATIONS

Preheat the fryer to 350°F. Dip escalopes in flour taking care to remove excess. Heat the pan with a little oil for a minute in the fryer, then spread the escalopes salted insert garlic and cook for 3 minutes, open and turn them upside down, also salt this side at this point give another 3 minutes of cooking time. Open again and put the wine in the pan, sprinkle with rosemary raise the temperature to 390°F and finish cooking for 3-4 minutes, until the sauce thickens. Plate by topping with the prosecco sauce that will have formed in the pan and a grating of pepper.

3 Meat specialities

Green pepper fillet

*Nutritional values:
Total protein 55.4 grams Total carbohydrates 6.1 grams
Total lipids 79.5 grams Total calories 961.5 kilocalories

SERVINGS: 2　　　PREP.TIME: 15 MIN　　　COOKING TIME : 6-8 MIN

INGREDIENTS

2 slices of tenderloin, approx. 1 inch thick
2 tbsp. pickled or fresh green peppercorns.
6,8 fl oz of cream
1 teaspoon Worchestershire sauce
Salt to taste.
Olive oil to taste.

INDICATIONS

In a small saucepan over low heat, reduce the cream slightly with the green peppercorns. When it has the consistency of a sauce, remove from the heat, add the Worchestershire sauce and adjust the salt. Preheat the air fryer to 350°F. Place the fillet in the basket, sprinkle with oil and salt. Cook for 3 minutes, then flip and cook for another 3 minutes (you can adjust the cooking time to your liking). Serve with the sauce on the side or covered with pepper sauce without removing the grains and fried potatoes.

3 Meat specialities

Beef tenderloin with prairie mushrooms

*Nutritional values:
Total protein 94.2 grams. Total carbohydrates 14.4 grams
Total lipids 11.8 grams. Total calories 540.8 kilocalories

SERVINGS: 2   PREP.TIME: 10 MIN   COOKING TIME : 10 MIN

INGREDIENTS

- 2 veal tenderloins (approx. 0,9 lbs)
- 2 tablespoons olive oil
- 1 clove of garlic, minced
- 7 oz of prataioli mushrooms or if you prefer champignons or others.
- Salt and pepper
- 1 baking pan

INDICATIONS

Preheat the fryer to 350°F. Remove the meat from the refrigerator half an hour before cooking to achieve even cooking. Cut the mushrooms large and put them in the pan with the fillets, olive oil, salt, pepper and garlic. Place the pan in the deep fryer. Set the timer to 10 minutes and cook the fillets until they are grilled and nicely colored, taking care to turn them upside down halfway through cooking and stir the mushrooms. Check that the mushrooms do not burn. Serve with a few green leaves and a side of potatoes.

3 Meat specialities

Stuffed pockets

*Nutritional values:
Total protein 77.9 grams Total carbohydrates 64.1 grams
Total lipids 27.4 grams Total calories 815.0 kilocalories

SERVINGS: 2   PREP.TIME: 15 MIN   COOKING TIME : 8 MIN

INGREDIENTS

4 thin slices of beef rump (0,7 lbs approx.)
4 thick slices of scamorza cheese (4,5 oz approx.)
4 slices of prosciutto
Crumbled taralli to taste
1 egg
Olive oil to taste.
Salt to taste.

INDICATIONS

Grind the taralli to a medium grain size. Beat the egg with the salt. Stuff the meat slices in half with provolone and prosciutto and fold in on themselves (dumpling closure). Dip the pockets in egg and then dip in ground taralli to make an even breadcrumb coating. Place the pockets on baking paper in the basket, spray with oil. Preheat the air fryer to 390°F and cook for the first 4 minutes, then remove the baking paper by flipping them over and cook for another 3-4 minutes.

"Vitello Tonnato"

***Nutritional values:**

Total Protein 178.6 grams Total Carbohydrates 2.1 grams
Total lipids 103.7 grams Total calories 1656.1 kilocalories

SERVINGS: 4   PREP.TIME: 15 MIN   COOKING: 20 MIN

INGREDIENTS

1,5 lbs roast
2 sprigs of fresh rosemary
Olive oil to taste.
Salt to taste.
SAUCE:
3,5 oz mayonnaise
3,5 oz tuna in olive oil
1 tablespoon capers
Black pepper

INDICATIONS

Preheat the air fryer to 390°F. Place the roast beef in the basket with the rosemary, cook by lowering the temperature to 325°F for 15 minutes, making sure to turn halfway through cooking. Remove from air fryer and cool before slicing. Meanwhile, in a blender, chop the tuna with the mayonnaise and capers until smooth; if you want it softer, add a drizzle of olive oil. Serve in thin slices with a spoonful of the resulting sauce spread over each slice. Great when cold, leave it for a couple of hours in the refrigerator before serving. Decorate with a few capers.

3 Meat specialities

Roast beef in pink dot

*Nutritional values:

Total Protein 161.4 grams Total Carbohydrates 60.5 grams
Total lipids 25.9 grams Total calories 1120.7 kilocalories

SERVINGS: 4   PREP.TIME: 20 MIN   COOKING TIME : 15 MIN

INGREDIENTS

1,5 lbs roast
2 sprigs of fresh rosemary
Olive oil to taste.
Salt to taste.
1 baking dish
FOR THE SAUCE:
4 large carrots
2 onions
1 celery branch
4 tablespoons olive oil

INDICATIONS

Preheat the air fryer to 395°F. Coarsely chop carrot, onion and celery and season with oil. Place the vegetables and roast in the pan, cook by lowering the temperature to 320°F for 15 minutes, making sure to turn halfway through cooking and with a spoon turn the bottom vegetables as well. Remove from air fryer and cool a few minutes before slicing. Meanwhile, collect the vegetables and cooking juices, blend in a blender and reduce a little in a pan over low heat, adjusting the salt. Serve sliced with a brush of the resulting sauce.

3 Meat specialities

Red Martini Beef

Nutritional values:
Total Protein 61.5 grams Total Carbohydrates 0.0 grams
Total lipids 20.0 grams Total calories 451.0 kilocalories

SERVINGS: 2-3   PREP.TIME: 10 MIN   COOKING : 12 MIN

INGREDIENTS

0,7 lbs of beef slices
1 tablespoon olive oil
3,4 fl oz of red Martini
1/2 teaspoon ground ginger
Salt and pepper to taste.
1 round baking dish 5,5 inches in diameter

INDICATIONS

Marinate the meat with martini, salt and ginger for about 30 minutes.
MARTINI SAUCE: Put the juice from the marinade in a saucepan to simmer. When the liquid has reduced by half, remove from the heat, adjust the salt.
Preheat the air fryer to 390°F. Spray the meat with a little oil. Place in the pan (the pan will collect all the cooking liquids). Place the pan in the basket in the air fryer. Set the timer to 12 minutes and cook until golden brown. Add the sauce and mix well, cook for another 3 minutes and serve. This is a great dish served with mashed potatoes.

3 Meat specialities

Mouthwatering meatballs

*Nutritional values:
Total protein 110.4 grams-Total carbohydrates 22.3 grams
Total lipids 42.1 grams-Total calories 909.0 kilocalories

SERVINGS: 3-4   PREP.TIME: 15 MIN   COOKING TIME : 8 MIN

INGREDIENTS

0,9lbs lean minced meat
1 tablespoon pecorino cheese
1 lightly beaten egg
Freshly ground pepper
3 tablespoons breadcrumbs
2 oz of salami or sausage, finely chopped
1 small onion, finely chopped

INDICATIONS

Preheat the air fryer to 390°F. In a bowl mix the ground meat with the egg, breadcrumbs, salami, onion, thyme, pecorino cheese 1 teaspoon salt and a good dose of pepper. Mix everything well, then with wet hands shape meatballs 5cm in diameter. Place the meatballs in the air fryer with a few splashes of oil. Set the timer to 8 minutes and roast, turning the meatballs a couple of times until they are well cooked and golden brown.

3 Meat specialities

Beef Bites with Red Martini

*Nutritional values:

**Total Protein 61.5 grams Total Carbohydrates 0.0 grams
Total lipids 20.0 grams Total calories 451.0 kilocalories**

SERVINGS: 2-3   PREP.TIME: 15 MIN   COOKING TIME : 12 MIN

INGREDIENTS

0,7 lbs beef tenderloin
1 tablespoon olive oil
3,4 fl oz of red Martini
1/2 teaspoon ground ginger
Salt and pepper to taste.
1 round baking dish 5,5 inches in diameter

INDICATIONS

Cut the tenderloin into small pieces and marinate the morsels with martini, salt and ginger for about 30 minutes. Place the juice from the marinade in a saucepan to simmer. When the liquid has reduced by half, remove from the heat, adjust the salt.

Preheat the air fryer to 390°F. Spray the morsels with a little oil. Place in the pan (the pan will collect all the cooking liquid). Place the pan in the basket in the air fryer. Set the timer to 9 minutes and cook until golden brown. Add the sauce and mix well, cook for another 3 minutes and serve.

3 Meat specialities

Fiorentina steak

*Nutritional values:
Total protein 87.2 grams Total carbohydrates 0.0 grams
Total lipids 28.8 grams Total calories 607.9 kilocalories

SERVINGS: 2   PREP.TIME: 10 MIN   COOKING TIME : 10 MIN

INGREDIENTS

1 bone-in steak 1-1,1 lbs
Salt to taste.
Black pepper to taste.
1/2 teaspoon garlic powder
1/2 teaspoon dehydrated onion
Dried oregano to taste.
Dried rosemary to taste.
Cayenne to taste.
Olive oil 0,5 fl oz approx.

INDICATIONS

Preheat air fryer to 390°F. Mix oil and spices and brush evenly over meat. Cook 3 minutes per side (rare) 5 minutes per side (medium). Let it rest for 3-4 minutes to get liquid distribution inside the meat, after which you can cut and enjoy it. You can get the most out of this recipe by applying seasoning to the meat 2-3 hours in advance and taking it out of the refrigerator 40 minutes before cooking.

Simple codfish "Baccalà"

Nutritional values:
Total Protein 52.3 grams Total Carbohydrates 0.0 grams
Total lipids 6.9 grams Total calories 270.8 kilocalories

SERVINGS: 2   PREP.TIME: 5 MIN   COOKING TIME : 6 MIN

INGREDIENTS

2 desalted cod fillets (0,7 lbs approx.)
Flour o qb.
Olive oil qb.
Salt and pepper to taste.
Parsley qb.

INDICATIONS

Preheat the fryer to 350°F.
Season fillets with salt and pepper on both, flour sides and sift to remove excess flour, spray with a little oil, place directly in oiled basket and cook for 5-6 minutes.
Serve with a sprinkling of fresh chopped parsley or a few strands of crispy fried onion.

Walnut-crusted salmon

Nutritional values:

Total protein 66.7 grams - Total carbohydrates 53.4 grams
Total lipids 71.1 grams - Total calories 1120.0 kilocalories

SERVINGS: 2   PREP.TIME: 10 MIN   COOKING TIME: 13 MIN

INGREDIENTS

- 2 slices of salmon (0,7 lbs)
- 2,2 oz of whole-grain breadcrumbs
- 2 oz of broken walnuts
- 1 tablespoon chopped parsley
- 1 lemon juice
- Salt to taste
- Olive oil to taste
- 1 tablespoon dried herbs (thyme, marjoram, sage)

INDICATIONS

Put the bread crumbs in a bowl, pour in the lemon juice and mix with the dried herbs and chopped walnuts. Salt the fillets and coat them with the bread mixture. Press lightly to make it stick. Drizzle with a little olive oil. Place in the basket and bake at 320°F for 10 minutes; complete roasting with another 2-3 minutes at 370°F. Remove from the oven and serve with a side dish to your liking.

4 Fish and Seafood

"Sicilian" Fried Stuffed Sardines

*Nutritional values:
Total Protein 95.0 grams Total Carbohydrates 120.5 grams
Total lipids 38.2 grams Total calories 1206.2 kilocalories

SERVINGS: 2   PREP.TIME: 20 MIN   COOKING TIME : 15 MIN

INGREDIENTS

- 0,7 lbs of fresh sardines
- 3,5 oz of breadcrumbs
- 1,5 oz of pecorino cheese
- 1 tablespoon chopped parsley
- 1/2 teaspoon hot chili pepper
- Type 0 flour qb.
- 1 egg
- Olive oil
- 1 lemon juice
- salt

INDICATIONS

Wash and dry the sardines. In a bowl mix the breadcrumbs, egg, pecorino cheese, parsley and chili pepper. Open the sardines and fill the belly with the breadcrumb mixture and roll the sardines in flour and remove the excess with a colander. Preheat the air fryer to 390°F. Place directly into the basket steaming with a little olive oil and cook for approx. 8 minutes. Turn them over gently and cook for about 6 minutes more. Serve topped with lemon juice.

4 Fish and Seafood

Inked cuttlefish

Nutritional values:
Total protein 42.5 grams-Total carbohydrates 2.6 grams
Total lipids 10.1 grams-Total calories 270.7 kilocalories

SERVINGS: 2   PREP.TIME: 10 MIN   COOKING TIME : 8 MIN

INGREDIENTS

0,7 lbs of cuttlefish strips
1 minced garlic tooth
1 tablespoon squid ink
6 fl oz of broth (vegetable or fish)
Olive oil and salt to taste
1 baking pan

INDICATIONS

You can use the ink from purchased cuttlefish, but if you bought them already cleaned you can buy a sachet of ink at the fish market. Preheat the fryer to 410°F. Cut the cuttlefish into strips and the tentacles into small pieces. In the pan mix all the ingredients well, place the pan in the basket and cook for 7 to 8 minutes, turning halfway through cooking. When opening be careful of steam escaping. Be careful not to overcook, if they overcook they will become tough. Cuttlefish should cook either the right amount of time or a long time, as they will harden and soften again after long cooking. Serve with a few croutons in a soup plate.

Tuna Ligurian style

Nutritional values:
Total Protein 89.7 grams Total Carbohydrates 19.9 grams
Total lipids 45.3 grams Total calories 844.3 kilocalories

SERVINGS: 4   PREP.TIME: 10 MIN   COOKING TIME : 10 MIN

INGREDIENTS

4 slices of bluefin tuna
0,9 lbs of cherry tomatoes
1 tablespoon capers
1,8 oz of pitted taggiasca olives
2 cloves of garlic slices
Olive oil to taste
4 tbsp. white wine
Fresh basil leaves to taste
Salt qb.
White pepper to taste.
1 baking pan

INDICATIONS

In the oiled baking dish arrange a base of rolled garlic, half the cherry tomatoes and a few basil leaves, then the fish slices seasoned with salt pepper and a few splashes of oil, finally top with the remaining tomato olives and capers. Drizzle with the wine. Preheat the fryer to 390°F and cook for 7 to 8 minutes. Serve with its garnish and the sauce collected in the pan.

Mussels au gratin with pecorino cheese

*Nutritional values:
Total protein 69.3 grams Total carbohydrates 9.4 grams
Total lipids 59.0 grams Total calories 846.9 kilocalories

SERVINGS: 2-3   PREP.TIME: 10 MIN   COOKING TIME: 5 MIN

INGREDIENTS

30 mussels
5,3 oz of lightly aged pecorino cheese
1 teaspoon of garlic powder
1 tablespoon chopped parsley

INDICATIONS

In a saucepan on the stove, cook the mussels with the lid on until they have opened. Drain them and remove half the shell, then mix the pecorino cheese, garlic and parsley.

Arrange the half-shells on the basket and in the center of each arrange a mussel. Using a teaspoon, coat the mussels with the cheese mixture, then moisten the surface with a few drops of the mussels' cooking water and spray with a little olive oil. Heat in the air fryer at 360°F for 2 to 3 minutes until golden brown.

4 Fish and Seafood

Salmon with dill

Nutritional values:
Total protein 46.0 grams Total carbohydrates 2.5 grams
Total lipids 35.0 grams Total calories 509.0 kilocalories

SERVINGS: 2   PREP.TIME: 5 MIN   COOKING TIME : 7 MIN

INGREDIENTS

2 slices of salmon
(9 oz approx.)
Salt qb.
Pepper to taste.
Olive oil a few splashes
1 tablespoon chopped fresh dill

INDICATIONS

Preheat the fryer to 350°F.
Place salmon in fryer with salt pepper, half the dill and a few splashes of oil, cook for 7 minutes making sure to turn once halfway through cooking. Remove from basket and plate, sprinkling dill over the surface.

4 Fish and Seafood

Warm shrimp and prawn salad

*Nutritional values:
Total protein 61.1 grams Total carbohydrates 30.7 grams
Total lipids 22.2 grams Total calories 567.2 kilocalories

SERVINGS: 4   PREP.TIME: 15 MIN   COOKING TIME : 15 MIN

INGREDIENTS

7 oz of cleaned shrimp tails
7 oz of cleaned langoustine tails
2 oz of sliced celery
1 green pepper
5,3 oz of diced tomato
3,5 oz of julienned red onion
2 oz of pitted olives
1 tablespoon capers
Chopped parsley
Salt to taste
Olive oil a few sprinkles
1 baking pan

INDICATIONS

Preheat the fryer to 375°F.
Slice the bell bell pepper into rounds and set aside. Place the rest of the ingredients excluding the shellfish and parsley in the pan in the fryer and cook for 5 minutes, finally add the shellfish mixing with the other ingredients and cook for 5 minutes. Insert the raw pepper out of the cooking time. You can serve hot taking care to arrange the vegetables on the plates as a bed and the shellfish placed on top with a sprinkling of fresh parsley.

4 Fish and Seafood

Whole-grain salmon gratin

Nutritional values:
Total Protein 44.3 grams Total Carbohydrates 50.5 grams
Total lipids 29.3 grams Total calories 642.9 kilocalories

SERVINGS: 2   PREP.TIME: 10 MIN   COOKING TIME: 13 MIN

INGREDIENTS

2 slices of salmon (7 oz)
3,5 oz of wholemeal breadcrumbs
1/2 lemon and peel in strips
salt
Olive oil
1 tablespoon dried herbs (thyme, marjoram, sage)

INDICATIONS

Place the breadcrumbs in a bowl, pour in the lemon juice and mix with the dried herbs and salt. Arrange the salmon on a baking sheet and cover it with the bread mixture. Press lightly to make it stick.
Drizzle with a little olive oil. Place in the basket and bake at 325°F for 10 minutes; complete toasting with another 2-3 minutes at 360°F. Remove from the oven and serve with a slice of lemon.

Sea bass baked in foil

Nutritional values:

Total protein 58.0 grams Total carbohydrates 2.5 grams
Total lipids 10.3 grams Total calories 334.7 kilocalories

SERVINGS: 2   PREP.TIME: 20 MIN   COOKING TIME : 30 MIN

INGREDIENTS

1 cleaned sea bass (bass) without head 0,7 lbs approx.
1 teaspoon dried herbs (fish mix)
1 clove of garlic, finely chopped
5 capers, finely chopped
1 teaspoon parsley
2 thin slices of lemon with peel
1 tablespoon white wine.
Salt to taste.
Baking paper
Food-grade foil

INDICATIONS

Dry the inside of the sea bass well after emptying it of its innards and rinsing it. Sprinkle herbs, garlic, capers, parsley and salt on baking paper. Brush a small amount of oil on one side and sprinkle with salt. Place a lemon slice on the paper and place the fish on top. Now season the other outer side of the fish. Lay the remaining lemon slice on top of the sea bass and douse the bottom with wine, then close the paper over itself. Wrap the first wrapper with 'kitchen foil, leaving a small slit at the top to allow excess steam to escape. Preheat the air fryer to 340°F. Place the wrapper in the basket and cook for 35 minutes.

4 Fish and Seafood

Crispy salmon fingers

Nutritional values:
Total Protein 99.9 grams Total Carbohydrates 104.3 grams
Total lipids 63.9 grams Total calories 1391.6 kilocalories

SERVINGS: 3-4   PREP.TIME: 10 MIN   COOKING TIME : 8-9 MIN

INGREDIENTS

- 0,9 lbs of salmon fillet
- Flour to taste.
- 2 eggs
- Breadcrumbs to taste
- 4 tablespoons corn flakes
- Salt and pepper to taste.
- Olive oil to taste.

INDICATIONS

Cut the salmon fillets into sticks about 1 inch thick. Beat the eggs with salt and pepper. Coat the sticks in flour, then egg, then coat with breadcrumbs mixed with hand-crushed corn flakes, making the breadcrumbs adhere well to the fillets. Preheat the air fryer to 350°F. Place the sticks in the basket and spray with a little oil. Cook for 4 minutes and then turn them over and cook another 4-5 minutes, until crispy. Serve with a squeeze of lime or lemon juice, along with a salad of arugula and tomatoes with balsamic vinegar.

4 Fish and Seafood

Crispy calamari

Nutritional values:

Total protein 47.2 grams Total carbohydrates 62.8 grams
Total lipids 9.9 grams Total calories 529.1 kilocalories

SERVINGS: 2   PREP.TIME: 10 MIN   COOKING TIME : 8 MIN

INGREDIENTS

- 0,7 lbs of fresh squid rings
- Olive oil to taste.
- Salt to taste.
- Type 0 wheat flour
- Chopped parsley
- Juice of 1 lemon

INDICATIONS

Dry the squid from the washing water, place them in a bowl and add the flour. Shake to coat them completely. Using a strainer, discard the excess flour. Spray the basket with oil and arrange the squid without overlapping (if there are too many, cook in several times). Spray some more oil on the squid. Bake at 395°F for 7 to 8 minutes. Serve on a plate, sprinkling with parsley and salt and drizzling with lemon juice.

Serve with a 'fennel salad.

4 Fish and Seafood

Roasted Sea Bass

*Nutritional values:
Total protein 49.9 grams Total carbohydrates 2.2 grams
Total lipids 9.6 grams Total calories 294.8 kilocalories

SERVINGS: 2   PREP.TIME: 5 MIN   COOKING TIME : 7 MIN

INGREDIENTS

2 fillets of sea bass 0,7 lbs approx.
1 tooth of minced garlic
1 teaspoon fresh or dried thyme
1 lemon
1 tablespoon parsley
Olive oil to taste.
Salt to taste.

INDICATIONS

Season the fillets with a little oil, salt and thyme. Preheat the fryer to 365°F. Arrange the fillets with the skin underneath and cook for 6-7 minutes without turning them.
Plate with a sprinkling of parsley and half a lemon on the plate.

Prawn quick skewers

***Nutritional values:**
Total Protein 64.3 grams Total Carbohydrates 34.6 grams
Total lipids 8.5 grams Total calories 472.2 kilocalories

SERVINGS: 2 PREP.TIME: 10 MIN COOKING TIME : 7 MIN

INGREDIENTS

- 16 medium prawns (1 lb)
- 16 halved cherry tomatoes
- 1 clove of garlic, minced
- 1 onion peeled into wedges
- 1 tablespoon parsley
- ½ teaspoon anise powder
- Black pepper to taste.
- Salt to taste.
- Olive oil a few sprinkles

INDICATIONS

In a bowl place 1 tablespoon olive oil, the aniseed salt garlic and pepper. Stir to flavor the prawns, onion squares and tomatoes and rest for a few minutes. Preheat the fryer to 365°F in the meantime assemble 4 skewers alternating vegetables and prawns. Cook for 6-7 minutes taking care to turn the skewers halfway through cooking.

4 Fish and Seafood

Scallops gratin

***Nutritional values:**
Total protein 37.5 grams Total carbohydrates 46.7 grams
Total lipids 21.3 grams Total calories 351.5 kilocalories

SERVINGS: 4   PREP.TIME: 10 MIN   COOKING TIME: 20 MIN

INGREDIENTS

- 8 Scallops
- Extra virgin olive oil
- Salt
- Pepper
- 2,2 oz of Breadcrumbs
- 1 tablespoon chopped parsley
- 1 tooth of minced garlic

INDICATIONS

Clean the shellfish, keep the middle part and the orange coral remove the rest.

Wash them well. Also save the shell for cooking and serving them.

Place the shells, on the baking sheet with a fruit inside each. Put 1 splash of extra virgin olive oil.

Season with salt and pepper.

Sprinkle with bread crumbs and minced garlic.

Bake at 360°F for about 20 minutes, until the scallop is au gratin. You can add a touch of color with chopped parsley.

4 Fish and Seafood

Calamari with stuffed heart

*Nutritional values:
Total Protein 91.4 grams Total Carbohydrates 158.8 grams
Total lipids 33.7 grams Total calories 1304.4 kilocalories

SERVINGS: 4   PREP.TIME: 10 MIN   COOKING TIME : 7-8 MIN

INGREDIENTS

- 4 medium squid (3,5 oz each approx.)
- 7 oz of breadcrumbs
- 1,5 oz of pecorino romano cheese
- 2 oz of chopped celery
- 5,5 oz of boiled rice
- 1,5 oz of anchovies in olive oil
- 2 tbsp. chopped parsley
- Olive oil to taste

INDICATIONS

Mix the breadcrumbs, celery, rice, pecorino, chopped anchovies and half the parsley with a tablespoon of olive oil. Fill the squid bellies by dividing the filling and lay on the basket, steaming with a little oil. At the temperature of 390°F cook the squid for 3 minutes, then turn them over and cook for another 3-4 minutes.
Serve hot with a nice fennel oil and lemon salad.

Italian-style cheesecake

Nutritional values:
Total Protein 63.2 grams Total Carbohydrates 260.8 grams
Total lipids 178.0 grams Total calories 2898.0 kilocalories

SERVINGS: 4   PREP.TIME: 25 MIN   COOKING TIME : 20 MIN

INGREDIENTS

- 1 lb of cream cheese
- 2 tbs of honey
- 5,3 oz of dry cookie crumbs
- ½ teaspoon vanilla extract
- 2 eggs, large
- 4,2 oz of sugar
- 2 tbsp. unsalted butter
- 1 baking sheet

INDICATIONS

Cut a piece of baking paper to line the bottom of the baking dish. Place it in the baking dish, mix together the crumbs with the butter and honey, spread over the bottom of the baking dish to create the base and press down a little to give it texture. Place the pan in the air fryer. Adjust the baking time to 4 minutes at 345°F. In a mixer, mix the cheese with the sugar. Add one egg at a time until creamy, finally include the vanilla and mix well. Remove the pan from the air fryer and pour the cheese mixture over the cookie crust. Place the cheesecake in the air fryer. Adjust the baking time to 15 minutes at 300°F. Chill for 3 hours in the refrigerator before serving. It will be great served with strawberry jam as a topping or any other fruit.

Blueberry muffins "Tortini"

***Nutritional values:**

Total protein 25.3 grams-Total carbohydrates 178.1 grams
Total lipids 58.1 grams-Total calories 1336.5 kilocalories

SERVINGS: **4**   PREP.TIME: **20** MIN   COOKING TIME : **15** MIN

INGREDIENTS

- 2,1 oz of butter
- 2 fl oz of fresh whole milk
- 5 oz of "oo"-type flour
- 2,1 oz of sugar
- 1 egg
- 1 pinch of baking powder
- ½ sachet of vanillin
- 2,5 oz of blueberries
- ¼ teaspoon baking soda
- 1 pinch of salt
- Baking tool: Muffin cups

INDICATIONS

Soften the room temperature butter in the bowl. Add the sugar and then beat vigorously until creamy. Add the egg, continuing to beat. Pour in the room temperature milk slowly, whisking until smooth and soft. Sift the flour into a bowl and mix it together with the baking powder, baking soda, vanillin and salt. Add them a little at a time to the mixture until it is creamy without lumps. Add the blueberries to the mixture. Preheat the air fryer to 365°F. Fill the ramekins two-thirds full with the mixture. Set the timer to 15 minutes and bake the muffins until lightly browned.

5 Sweet Cakes and Biscuits

Peach cupcakes

Nutritional values:

Total Protein 32.4 grams Total Carbohydrates 199.6 grams
Total lipids 105.3 grams Total calories 1875.8 kilocalories

SERVINGS: 4   PREP.TIME: 20 MIN   COOKING TIME: 15 MIN

INGREDIENTS

- 3,5 oz of flour
- 2,5 fl oz of olive oil
- 3,5 oz of sugar
- 1 egg + 1 yolk
- 1 pinch of baking powder
- 3 peaches, peeled and diced
- 2 teaspoons chopped almonds
- Vanilla.
- Muffin cups

INDICATIONS

In a planetary mixer or with electric whips, beat the eggs with the sugar. Sift the flour and baking powder and add to the mixture in 2 to 3 times, add the oil and finally the 3 peaches.

Preheat the air fryer to 355°F. Place the batter in the ramekins and sprinkle with the chopped almonds. Bake, lowering the temperature to 320°F for 12 to 15 minutes depending on the size of the cups. Cool and serve. They go well with ice cream or a mascarpone cream.

Egg pudding "Budino"

Nutritional values:

Total protein 33.4 grams Total carbohydrates 144.5 grams
Total lipids 28.4 grams Total calories 966.9 kilocalories

SERVINGS: 6   PREP.TIME: 20 MIN   COOKING TIME: 20 MIN

INGREDIENTS

- 13,5 fl oz of milk
- 3 eggs
- 4,2 oz of sugar
- 2 tablespoons dry white wine
- 1/2 lemon peel in strips
- Vanilla
- Aluminum pudding cups

INDICATIONS

Bring to boil in a saucepan, milk, sugar, wine, lemon zest and vanilla. Remove from heat and discard lemon zest. Add eggs with a whisk and mix well but without incorporating air. Let steep for 5 minutes. Preheat the air fryer to 300°F. Pour the mixture into the molds and place in the basket. Lower the temperature to 250°F and bake for approx. 30-35 minutes until a dark crust and a slight rise in mass are obtained. Cool for 2 hours in the refrigerator and serve on a plate with a sauce of your choice or hot chocolate.

5 Sweet Cakes and Biscuits

Cocoa and Chocolate Drop Cake

*Nutritional values:
Total protein 58.9 grams- Total carbohydrates 330.0 grams
Total lipids 98.8 grams- Total calories 2443.8 kilocalories

SERVINGS: 4   PREP.TIME: 20 MIN   COOKING TIME : 25 MIN

INGREDIENTS

- 3 eggs
- 3,5 oz of sugar
- 7,8 oz of flour
- 1,2 oz of cocoa
- 1,7 fl oz of milk
- 1,5 fl oz of sunflower seed oil
- 0,3 oz of baking powder
- 3,5 oz of dark chocolate chips
- 8,5 inches baking pan

INDICATIONS

In a planetary mixer or with electric whips, beat the eggs. Slowly add the oil and milk. At low speed incorporate the sifted flour, baking powder and cocoa, finally the chocolate chips. Pour the mixture into the greased baking dish. Bake in the preheated air fryer at 320°F for 15 minutes and then increase the temperature to 365°F for another 10 minutes. Test with a stick to be sure of baking.

Cream burned

Nutritional values:

Total protein 39.1 grams-Total carbohydrates 221.3 grams
Total lipids 176.8 grams-Total calories 2561.0 kilocalories

SERVINGS: 6   PREP.TIME: 20 MIN   COOKING TIME : 20 MIN

INGREDIENTS

4 eggs
1/2 liter of cream
3,4 fl oz of milk
6,2 oz of sugar
Vanilla powder 1 sachet
6 Baking pudding cups

INDICATIONS

In a small saucepan, boil the cream, milk, sugar and vanilla.
Add the eggs off the heat. Preheat the air fryer to 390°F. Pour the mixture into the pudding molds. Place them in the fryer and bake at 320°F for 15 to 20 minutes, depending on the size of the molds. It will be ready when it has solidified and a crust has formed. Cool in the refrigerator and cover with a spoonful of sugar that you can burn with a blowtorch or in a grill. You can use the deep fryer to grate it. Serve with ice cream.

Big milk donut "Ciambella"

Nutritional values:

Total protein 48.4 grams Total carbohydrates 236.7 grams
Total lipids 6.3 grams Total calories 1196.9 kilocalories

SERVINGS: 4   PREP.TIME: 20 MIN   COOKING TIME: 35 MIN

INGREDIENTS

- 7 oz of egg whites
- 2,2 oz of sugar
- 4 fl oz of milk
- 7 oz of flour
- 0,3 oz of baking powder
- 3 tablespoons granulated sugar
- A 8 inches doughnut mold

INDICATIONS

In a planetary mixer or with electric whips beat the egg whites and sugar to stiff peaks, then at low speed add the sifted flour and baking powder a little at a time. When the mixture is smooth, add the milk, beating at low speed. Pour into the buttered and floured mold.

On the surface sprinkle granulated sugar. In the air fryer at 305°F, bake for approx. 35 minutes. If you want a firmer browning, increase the temperature a little in the last few minutes.

Burnt Coffee Cream

Nutritional values:

Total Protein 37.0 grams Total Carbohydrates 201.3 grams
Total lipids 180.3 grams Total calories 2577.0 kilocalories

SERVINGS: 4   PREP.TIME: 20 MIN   COKING TIME : 20 MIN

INGREDIENTS

- 4 eggs
- 1/2 liter of cream
- 6,2 oz of sugar
- Vanilla powder 1 sachet
- 4 fl oz of strong coffee
- 6 Baking pudding cups

INDICATIONS

In a small saucepan, boil the cream, coffee, sugar and vanilla. Add the eggs off the heat. Preheat the air fryer to 390°F. Pour the mixture into the pudding molds. Place them in the fryer and bake at 160°C for 15 to 20 minutes, depending on the size of the molds. It will be ready when it has solidified and formed a "burnt" crust. Great served cold with a scoop of vanilla ice cream. After chilling in the refrigerator, you can sprinkle a little sugar on the crust and burn it with a kitchen torch or grate it in the deep fryer 1 to 2 minutes.

Sicilian orange and ricotta cake

Nutritional values:

Total Protein 72.4 grams Total Carbohydrates 363.7 grams
Total lipids 124.2 grams Total calories 2861.1 kilocalories

SERVINGS: 6   PREP.TIME: 20 MIN   COOKING TIME : 45 MIN

INGREDIENTS

9,2 oz of flour
8,8 oz of ricotta cheese
3 eggs
5,3 oz of sugar
2,7 fl oz of sunflower seed oil
0,4 oz of vanilla baking powder
1 pinch of salt
grated peel of one orange
A cake pan 8 inches in diameter

INDICATIONS

In a planetary mixer or with electric whips, beat the eggs, sugar, and salt. When they have reached a frothy consistency, add the oil and then the ricotta, still whipping. Finally incorporate the flour, baking powder and orange peel. Preheat the air fryer to 365°F. Pour the mixture into the buttered and floured pan and bake for about 40-45 minutes, taking care to open the basket slightly after 30 minutes to let the moisture escape. Repeat the opening after 5 minutes.
Let cool and rest in the refrigerator for 2 hours and serve cold with fresh berries.

Caprese Cake

Nutritional values:
Total Protein 61.7 grams Total Carbohydrates 279.9 grams
Total lipids 87.7 grams Total calories 2155.4 kilocalories

SERVINGS: **4** PREP.TIME: **20** MIN COOKING TIME : **25** MIN

INGREDIENTS

- 3 eggs
- 3,5 oz of sugar
- 7,8 oz of flour
- 1,1 oz of cocoa
- 1,7 fl oz of milk
- 1,5 oz of sunflower seed oil
- 0,3 oz of baking powder
- 3,5 oz of rolled almonds
- 1 8,5 inches of baking pan

INDICATIONS

In a planetary mixer or with electric whips, beat the eggs. Slowly add the oil and milk. At low speed incorporate the sifted flour, baking powder and cocoa. Pour the mixture into the greased baking dish and sprinkle with the almonds. Bake in the preheated air fryer at 320°F for 15 minutes and then increase the temperature to 365°F for another 10 minutes. Test with a stick to make sure they are cooked.

Coffee italian cheesecake

Nutritional values:

Total protein 63.2 grams-Total carbohydrates 260.8 grams
Total lipids 178.0 grams-Total calories 2898.0 kilocalories

SERVINGS: 4   PREP.TIME: 20 MIN   COOKING TIME: 20 MIN

INGREDIENTS

- 1 lb of cream cheese
- 2 tbsp. ground coffee
- 2 tbsp of honey
- 5,3 oz of dry cookie crumbs
- ½ teaspoon vanilla extract
- 2 eggs, large
- 4,3 oz of sugar
- 2 tbsp. unsalted butter
- 1 baking sheet

INDICATIONS

Cut a piece of baking paper to line the bottom of the baking dish. Place it in the baking dish, mix together the crumbs with the butter and honey, spread over the bottom of the baking dish to create the base and press down a little to give it texture. Place the pan in the air fryer. Adjust the baking time to 4 minutes at 345°F. In a mixer, mix the cheese with the sugar. Add one egg at a time until creamy, finally include the vanilla, coffee and mix well. Remove the pan from the air fryer and pour the cheese mixture over the cookie crust. Place the cheesecake in the air fryer. Adjust the baking time to 15 minutes at 300°F. Chill for 3 hours in the refrigerator before serving.

Carnival fritters "Frittelle"

Nutritional values:

Total Protein 24.1 grams Total Carbohydrates 187.4 grams
Total lipids 41.3 grams Total calories 1217.3 kilocalories

SERVINGS: 2-3   PREP.TIME: 20 MIN   COOKING TIME : 6-7 MIN

INGREDIENTS

1 egg
5,3 oz of flour
1,5 oz of sugar
Icing sugar to taste
1,2 fl oz of sunflower oil
1 tablespoon "strega" liqueur (or anise or rum)
1 pinch of salt
Vanilla to taste
1 teaspoon baking powder
Olive oil for cooking to taste

INDICATIONS

In a bowl mix the oil, egg, flour, baking powder, liqueur the vanilla and salt. When you get a workable dough, let it rest in the refrigerator for 30 minutes. Remove from the refrigerator and cut into pieces of 20 g each. Roll the dough with your hands to make 15 balls, place them in the basket on baking paper greased with oil and bake at 395°F for 3 minutes. Turn them over, drizzle with a little oil and bake for another 3-4 minutes until golden brown. Once cooked, sprinkle with powdered sugar. Depending on the fryer model, it may be convenient to bake them in two times to keep a good distance between them and cook them well. Serve them hot with a glass of sweet wine.

Eggless chocolate cookies

Nutritional values:

Total Protein 25.3 grams Total Carbohydrates 182.0 grams
Total lipids 112.6 grams Total calories 1841.0 kilocalories

SERVINGS: PREP.TIME: 20 MIN   COOKING TIME : 6 MIN

INGREDIENTS

1,1 oz of cocoa powder
1,8 oz of brown sugar
4,4 oz of flour
2,2 oz of chopped dark chocolate
2 teaspoons of vanilla baking powder
1 pinch of salt
3,5 oz of butter at room temperature
Baking paper

INDICATIONS

Mix the ingredients until smooth, form into balls and crush them lightly to make circles about 2 inches in diameter and 0.5 inch thick. Preheat the deep fryer to 390°F. Place the cookies on baking paper 2 cm apart and bake, lowering the temperature to 370°F Bake for 5-6 minutes. Peel off the paper once cool. Serve dusted with powdered sugar.

Spelt and raisin cookies

Nutritional values:
Total Protein 46.6 grams Total Carbohydrates 353.3 grams
Total lipids 103.2 grams Total calories 2527.5 kilocalories

SERVINGS: PREP.TIME: 20 MIN COOKING TIME : 15 MIN

INGREDIENTS

- 3,8 oz of butter
- 4,8 oz of brown sugar
- 2,2 oz of raisins
- 1 egg
- 8,8 oz of spelt flour
- 1 pinch of salt

INDICATIONS

Mix the ingredients together until smooth. Make a roll, cover with plastic wrap and let it rest in the refrigerator for 1 hour. Roll out the mass with a rolling pin to a thickness of about half an inch. Decorate with cookie cutters or cut squares with a knife. Preheat the air fryer to 350°F. Arrange cookies on a baking sheet with baking paper and bake for approx. 15 minutes. Remove from the oven when golden brown and allow to cool before consuming.

Dairy biscuits

Nutritional values:

Total Protein 36.5 grams Total Carbohydrates 331.7 grams
Total lipids 99.0 grams Total calories 2363.9 kilocalories

SERVINGS: PREP.TIME: 20 MIN   COOKING TIME : 10 MIN

INGREDIENTS

- 3,8 oz of butter
- 4,7 oz of white sugar
- 1 egg
- 8,8 oz of flour
- 1 pinch of salt
- 1 pinch of vanilla baking powder

INDICATIONS

Mix the ingredients together until smooth. Make a roll, cover with plastic wrap and let it rest in the refrigerator for 1 hour. Roll out the mass with a rolling pin to a thickness of about half an inch. Decorate with cookie cutters or cut squares with a knife. Preheat the air fryer to 350°F. Arrange cookies on a baking sheet with baking paper and bake for approx. 10 minutes. Remove from the oven when lightly browned and allow to cool before consuming. You can consume them as they are or dusted with powdered sugar.

Cocoa and hazelnut cookies

Nutritional values:

Total Protein 33.6 grams Total Carbohydrates 363.8 grams
Total lipids 108.1 grams Total calories 2563.0 kilocalories

SERVINGS: PREP.TIME: 20 MIN COOKING TIME : 8 MIN

INGREDIENTS

- 7 oz of sugar
- 5,3 oz of flour
- 2,8 oz of chopped hazelnuts
- 1,4 oz of bitter cocoa chips
- 2 teaspoons of vanilla baking powder
- 1 pinch of salt
- 1,8 oz of butter at room temperature
- Baking paper

INDICATIONS

Mix the ingredients together until smooth. Cut and form into balls and flatten them slightly to make circles about 2 inches in diameter and 2 inches high. Preheat the air fryer to 390°F. Arrange the cookies on baking paper 2 cm apart and bake, lowering the temperature to 365°F. Bake for 6 to 8 minutes.

5 Sweet Cakes and Biscuits

Sweet and savory crumble

Nutritional values:
Total protein 17.3 grams - Total carbohydrates 169.4 grams
Total lipids 84.5 grams - Total calories 1506.5 kilocalories

SERVINGS: PREP.TIME: 20 MIN   COOKING TIME : 15 MIN

INGREDIENTS

- 5,3 oz of flour
- 3,5 oz of soft butter
- 1,8 oz of brown sugar
- 0,18 oz of salt

INDICATIONS

Mix ingredients by hand or in planetary mixer without kneading too much and spread evenly on baking paper in basket. Preheat the deep fryer to 400°F. Insert the basket and bake for 12 to 15 minutes. It is excellent crumbled for cheesecake bottoms or spoon desserts. This crisp is suitable for some types of parfaits, but if you want variations, just add spices while keeping the proportions. It is also used as a crumb topping for ice cream.

Peanut Cookies

Nutritional values:
Total protein 29.3 grams-Total carbohydrates 206.2 grams
Total lipids 121.3 grams-Total calories 2033.1 kilocalories

SERVINGS: PREP.TIME: 20 MIN   COOKING TIME : 6-7 MIN

INGREDIENTS

- 2,1 oz of sugar
- 5,3 oz of flour
- 2,8 oz of roasted peanut granules
- 2 teaspoons vanilla baking powder
- 3,5 oz of butter at room temperature
- Baking paper

INDICATIONS

Combine ingredients (without peanuts) until smooth. Rest in the refrigerator about 20 minutes. Shape into balls and crush them lightly to make circles approx. 2 inches in diameter and 0,2 inches thick, cover with peanuts, press lightly with your hand to set them well on the surface. Preheat the air fryer to 390°F. Arrange the cookies on baking paper 1 cm apart and bake, lowering the temperature to 355°F. Bake for 6 to 7 minutes.

5 Sweet Cakes and Biscuits

Lady's Kisses "Baci di Dama"

**Nutritional values:*
Total Protein 33.0 grams Total Carbohydrates 246.0 grams
Total lipids 180.9 grams Total calories 2744.1 kilocalories

SERVINGS: PREP.TIME: 20 MIN   COOKING TIME : 7-8 MIN

INGREDIENTS

- 2,8 oz of hazelnut flour
- 3,5 oz of butter
- 0,7 oz of cocoa powder
- 3,5 oz of flour
- 3,5 oz of sugar
- 3,5 oz of hazelnut cream spread

INDICATIONS

Mix the flours, cocoa, butter and sugar by hand and let rest for 1 hour in the refrigerator. Form into balls about 2 centimeters in diameter and place them on baking paper in the basket lined with baking paper spaced apart. Preheat the air fryer to 350°F. Insert the basket and lower the temperature to 320°F. Cook for 7 to 8 minutes until lightly browned hemispheres have formed. Remove the basket and cool before touching them; hot they are very crumbly. Combine the half spheres with a teaspoon of spreadable cream (Nutella or similar) in the center. Rest for 2 hours before consuming.

5 Sweet Cakes and Biscuits

Sicilian Almond Pastries

*Nutritional values:
Total protein 39.4 grams Total carbohydrates 163.7 grams
Total lipids 83.0 grams Total calories 1558.9 kilocalories

SERVINGS: PREP.TIME: 20 MIN   COOKING TIME : 4-5 MIN

INGREDIENTS

5,3 oz of almond flour
5,3 oz of sugar
2 fresh egg whites
1/2 grated orange peel
Whole almonds for garnish

INDICATIONS

By hand with a wooden spoon or spatula, mix sugar and flour, adding lemon juice and egg white a little at a time (no need to use all of it, sometimes it turns out to be too much), until you get a soft but not liquid dough, from which you can make flakes with a pastry bag about 1 inch in diameter. Lay them on baking paper and leave 0,5 inch between each one. Place a whole almond in the center of each by pressing down. Let stand for 2 to 3 hours in the air at room temperature. Preheat the fryer to 395°F.
Cook for 4-5 minutes until golden brown, and once cool, remove from paper. Enjoy them with a good marsala wine.

5 Sweet Cakes and Biscuits

Crunchy hazelnut cookies

*Nutritional values:
Total protein 25.0 grams-Total carbohydrates 269.5 grams
Total lipids 86.5 grams-Total calories 1957.0 kilocalories

SERVINGS: PREP.TIME: **20** MIN   COOKING TIME : **10** MIN

INGREDIENTS

- 8,9 oz of Sugar
- 3,5 oz of hazelnut flour
- 1,5 oz of hazelnut kernels
- 2 egg whites

INDICATIONS

Combine the sugar and hazelnut flour. Add the egg whites, a little at a time, so as not to overdo it, as the dough should be soft but not runny. Mix in the crumbs. Line the basket with baking paper and use a spoon to place balls of 1 inch in diameter 0,5 inches apart. Preheat the air fryer to 365°F. Insert the basket and cook at 320°F until they puff up and reach a dry texture and consistent browning (about 8-10 minutes). Great with milk, but also with dry white wine.

Walnut cookies

Nutritional values:

Total Protein 26.5 grams Total Carbohydrates 182.5 grams
Total lipids 131.1 grams Total calories 2015.3 kilocalories

SERVINGS: PREP.TIME: 20 MIN   COOKING TIME : 5-6 MIN

INGREDIENTS

- 2,1 oz of sugar
- 5,3 oz of flour
- 2,8 oz of chopped walnuts
- 2 teaspoons vanilla baking powder
- 1 pinch of salt
- 3,5 oz of butter at room temperature
- Baking paper

INDICATIONS

Mix the ingredients together until smooth. Form into balls and crush them lightly to make circles about 2 inches in diameter and 1 inch thick. Preheat the air fryer to 392°F. Arrange the cookies on baking paper 1 cm apart and bake, lowering the temperature to 355°F. Bake for 5 to 6 minutes. These are eggless cookies so very crumbly, wait until they are well chilled before withdrawing them from the baking paper.

*Nutritional Values:

In this book at the end of each recipe the nutritional values of the same are given, the calculation does not refer to the individual portion, but to the total amount of the ingredients listed, since then everyone decides how many portions to make from a preparation, the indication of portions is always relative anyway, considering that a dish can be served as a taster, appetizer or main course. For those readers who need to have timely information on the nutritional values of the quantity they ingest, it will be sufficient to divide the values given by the number of servings obtained from the indicated quantities. It should also be said that the values reflect the foods specified in the recipe, if you change the type of cheese or sausage for example or exceed with oil etc. any change you give to the recipe will make the given values unreliable. However, the values given are calculated with the help of standard nutritional tables available online or in the nutritional media of common magazines. They constitute an indicative data that is always greatly appreciated by those who like to take care of their diet by monitoring their intake of calories and whatnot, avoiding time-consuming research and calculations for the users of the cookbook.

Use of the air fryer:

The air fryer, differs from normal fryers due to the use of hot air, which makes it much more similar to an oven although with much faster cooking, this is due to the confined cooking space, this substantial difference from the oven, allows the cooking of much less fatty and healthier foods, surpassing in speed even the normal immersion fryers, but avoiding the toxicity of overcooked and burned oils thanks to lower temperatures and without impregnating the food with oil, but producing the same crispness and flavor of a traditional fried food. The lower consumption of oil, also turns out to be an ecological contribution to the preparation of your dishes which will make them healthier for the entire ecosystem as well.

Tips and tricks for cooking:

- Some air fryers also get very hot externally during use. Pay attention to the suitability of the surface on which you place it. It is useful, for example, to place it on an oven rack, so as to improve ventilation and allow heat to disperse.

- In some recipes you will find the advice to resort to baking paper, always keep in mind that if it is not well secured to the basket (covered by the food and without excess parts that can wave), it could touch the heating element, burning, also it could reduce the speed of cooking, to obviate the problems in this regard is sufficient to buy the perforated baking paper that is produced specifically for air frying and that you find everywhere now. You can also make use of silicone mats created for the same purpose.

- For sweet preparations or otherwise requiring baking containers, you can also use disposable aluminum baking pans, cups etc. or the corresponding high temperature silicone ones.

- When first turned on, these appliances can give off unpleasant, plastic or otherwise unpleasant food preparation odors. There are some tricks to solve this problem. It is possible to prepare a solution of baking soda (2 teaspoons in a glass of water) and put it in an oven bowl inside the fryer, set it to cook at 180°C for 10 minutes checking that it does not dry out completely, this way the smell will be absorbed and eliminated. Putting a lemon cut in half and a sprig of rosemary can also perform the same function, 180°C for 10 minutes, making sure to bind the rosemary so that it does not fly into the heating elements.

- In the preparation of some fatty foods or even if they are overly seasoned, you may experience the production of fumes inside the fryer, this is due to the fact that the dripping fats dry on the bottom of the outer basket of the cooking chamber and burning generates fumes. To solve this problem, simply put a little water on the bottom of the outer basket, without overdoing it, but it should be enough to keep the drips that fall into it from burning.

- Never put excess oil on your food, use a steamer and good olive oil, in a limited amount, this will allow you to prepare much healthier, dietary and economical food.

- However, make sure to lightly grease the basket in order to prevent food from sticking.
- As for preheating the fryer, considerations must be made: some foods need an immediate heat shock, others do not. An already high temperature at the beginning of cooking allows for crispness, but beware: some foods may remain raw inside. For cooking a whole chicken for example, or for any other thick food that needs to cook well in the center, it is best not to preheat. For cakes and yeast products, it is best to avoid, extending cooking time and allowing the base to cook optimally.

- Precooked frozen foods, vegetables and small foods succeed more crisply by preheating the air fryer.

- Always cook by leaving the grill in the basket, allowing air to circulate well will also prevent excess oil in your preparations and ensure crispiness.

- Visually check the cooking, from time to time open the fryer and shake the basket or turn the food, this is also to see if it is cooking well, especially the first few times in familiarizing yourself with the appliance. You can take out the basket at any time to check the cooking, just close it well to restart the fryer, some models include a pause function.

- Usually in the instruction manual you will find some tables for cooking times, it is recommended to take a look at them, keep in mind that times and also temperatures are very different from immersion fryers, usually cooking at lower temperatures with reduced times.

- Do not overfill the basket, to allow room for the hot air to circulate and not compromise the cooking and crispiness of the food.

- With this appliance you will be able to grill and roast as well as fry foods.

- When cooking, never leave the fryer against the wall; it needs to have free air intake.

- Avoid cooking products that can splatter and stick to the heating elements (e.g., popcorn), in some cases it may even cause a fire.

Cleaning and maintenance:

- Usually in the manual provided by the manufacturer you will find directions for cleaning and maintaining your deep fryer, below are some tips from the author that are generally suitable for all models available on the market.

- Always let it cool down before starting cleaning and always unplug it from the power supply.

- A damp cloth will suffice for cleaning the outside.

- Basket and pan should be washed with dish soap and water, usually the moving parts are all dishwasher safe.

- Interior cleaning should be done with a sponge and warm water.

- Use a toothbrush to remove residual bits of food; do not risk scratching the nonstick coating with sharp utensils or abrasive sponges. For more tenacious dirt, moisten the part and let it soften a few minutes before scrubbing.

- Dry the various parts well with a kitchen cloth before reassembling them.

- The heating element also needs to be cleaned after each firing, make sure to do its cleaning only once it is well chilled and clean it with a damp cloth and very gently, in the case of more tenacious dirt moisten and scrub with a soft bristle brush. For drying the heating element, the action of an ordinary kitchen paper will be sufficient.

INDICATIVE TABLE OF AIR COOKING
STANDARD COOKING TIMES

THESE TIMES ARE INDICATIVE AND REFER TO ALL AIRFRYER MODELS ON THE MARKET. IT IS RECOMMENDED THAT YOU DO SOME TRIALS TO FAMILIARIZE YOURSELF WITH YOUR OWN.

FOOD	TEMPERATURE	TIMES IN THE AIR FRYER
MEAT AND FISH		
BACON	390°F	15 min
PORK RIBS	390°F	25 min
WHOLE CHICKEN	390°F	30 min
HAMBURGER	355°F	8-10 min
CHICKEN BREAST	390°F	20 min
CHICKEN WINGS	390°F	14-16 min
CHICKEN THIGHS	390°F	25 min
SEA BREAM	355°F	15 min
BACCALA'	355°F	10 min
SALMON	390°F	15 min
ROAST BEEF	390°F	45 min
PORK CHOPS	390°F	20 min
LAMB CUTLETS	390°F	20 min

MEAT BALLS	390 F	15 min
PRAWNS	320 F	8 min
BEEF TENDERLOIN	390 F	15 min
MEATLOAF	375 F	35 min
VEGETABLES		
ASPARAGUS	355 F	8 min
FRESH POTATOES	390 F	35 min
BROCCOLI	355 F	20 min
ARTICHOKES	390 F	20-30 min
DICE PUMPKIN	390 F	15-20 min
CARROTS	375 F	20 min
FENNEL	355 F	15-20 min
FROZEN FRENCH BEANS	355 F	12 min
PEPPERS	390 F	20 min
AUBERGINES	390 F	20 min
COURGETTES IN ROUNDS	375 F	20 min

FROZEN FOOD		
FRENCH FRIES	390 °F	15-20 min
SOFFICINI	355 °F	15 min
FAST CHICKEN	390 °F	12 min
SPINACH CUTLETS	390 °F	15 min
FISH FINGERS	360 °F	15 min
POTATO CROQUETTES	390 °F	15-20 min
CAKES AND BREADS		
BRIOCHES	320 °F	25-30 min
COOKIES	320 °F	10 min
MUFFIN	320 °F	12-15 min
SMALL BUTTER BREAD	375 °F	15-25 min
MINI PIZZAS	390 °F	8 min

Since this book does not refer to any specific air fryer model, it is up to the user to vary the cooking times and amounts of food used depending on the air fryer used, keeping in mind that variations in times are almost nonexistent, while those in cooking chamber volume can be quite different. In some cases, when the exact ingredient suggested cannot be found, you can refer to compatible substitutes. A classic example is cheese: you can substitute parmesan for a grated cheese of your choice, and melting cheeses such as camambert for a similar product. However, to achieve an authentic Italian flavor, I recommend using certified products whose origin guarantees a perfect result, as well as using the products indicated in the recipe to achieve the authentic flavor of the recipe.

WELL, I HOPE YOU HAVE REACHED THE END OF THIS BOOK SATISFIED WITH THE RECIPES YOU HAVE FOUND, I AM SURE YOU WILL GET GREAT RESULTS WITH THEM. IF YOU HAVE ANY ADVICE, QUESTIONS OR REQUESTS FOR ME, I WILL BE GLAD TO PERSONALLY READ YOUR E-MAILS, WHICH YOU CAN SEND TO:

artinaction56@gmail.com

If you enjoyed this book, I would love to read your review on the sales page, also to help other readers choose the book best suited to their needs.

Legal Note.

The contents and information in this book are in no way a substitute for any medical, legal, or financial advice that may be needed. The contents of this document are expressed for educational and recreational purposes and are from sources believed to be reliable based on the author's experience and beliefs. However, the author cannot guarantee its accuracy or validity and therefore cannot be held responsible for any errors or omissions. Therefore, before using the remedies or techniques suggested in this book, a professional (physician, lawyer, etc.) should be consulted. Use of this book indemnifies the author against any damages, costs, or expenses related to the use of the information or techniques contained herein. This disclaimer applies to any loss, damage, or injury caused by the application of the contents of this book, directly or otherwise, in breach of contract, tort, negligence, personal injury, criminal intent, or under any circumstances. The reader accepts all risks associated with and arising from the use of the information contained in this book. You also agree to seek professional advice if necessary (including, but not limited to, your physician, attorney, financial advisor, or other professional) before using the remedies, techniques, or information contained in this book.

Printed in Great Britain
by Amazon